THE LIFE & REGIMEN OF

THE BLESSED & HOLY SYNCLETICA

BY PSEUDO-ATHANASIUS

PART ONE:
ENGLISH TRANSLATION
BY ELIZABETH BRYSON BONGIE

Wipf & Stock
PUBLISHERS
Eugene, Oregon

Wipf and Stock Publishers
199 W 8th Ave, Suite 3
Eugene, OR 97401

The Life and Regimen of the Blessed and Holy Syncletica, Part One
The Translation
By Pseudo-Athanasius
Copyright©2003 Peregrina Publishing Co.
ISBN: 1-59752-443-3
Publication date 11/1/2005
Previously published by Peregrina Publishing Co., 2003

CONTENTS

✳

Introduction	5
Translation	9
References & Abbreviations	71
Notes	75
Select Bibliography	85
List of illustrations	93

18. *Sancta Syncletica.*

INTRODUCTION

At the present time the sole source of our knowledge of Syncletica is Pseudo-Athanasius' *The Life and Regimen of the Holy and Blessed Teacher Syncletica*. Chapters 4–21 and 103–113 of this fifth-century work give a few details of her life, while Chapters 22–102 present her teachings on the ascetic practices of a female desert anchorite.

The pervasive influence on Syncletica's thought of Evagrius Ponticus (346–399) places her in the last part of the fourth century at the earliest, while scholarly consensus places the composition of *The Life and Regimen* in the fifth century. The common attribution to Athanasius of this work is manifestly false for reasons of style and content, but two other possible authors are mentioned in some manuscripts – an ascetic Polycarp and an Arsenius of Pegades, both otherwise unknown.

Syncletica was born in Alexandria into a distinguished Christian family of Macedonian origin. Her two brothers died prematurely, one in childhood, the other shortly before his marriage; her sister was blind. Syncletica's parents wished her, as the only remaining eligible offspring, to take a husband from among her many suitors and to carry on the family line. She, however, from an early age had chosen a life of chastity and austerity. As soon as her parents died and she was free to follow her own inclinations, she distributed the family wealth among the poor, cut off her hair as a sign of her consecrated life as a virgin in the tradition of Thecla and, taking her sister with her, withdrew to a family tomb outside of Alexandria to live the life of a desert anchorite. The reputation of her holiness spread and eventually numbers of women gathered around her to learn her spiritual secrets. With the greatest reluctance she was persuaded to share her spiritual practices and insights with her disciples. It is the memories of these women that served as the major source for the author of the *Life and Regimen*. In her eightieth year she was smitten with a hideous degenerative disease, probably cancer. After three and a half years of heroic suffering, she finally passed to her reward amidst visions of angels, holy maidens, radiant light, and paradisal realms.

Although an account of Syncletica's life and teachings was written not long after her death, it languished, largely unread, through the centuries except for those passages selected by the compilers of the various collections of *The Sayings of the Desert Fathers*. The spiritual wisdom of only three women – Sarah, Theodora, and Syncletica – was deemed worthy of inclusion by these connoisseurs of desert spirituality. Of these three, Syncletica's teachings are the most extensively represented. Through the translation of these Sayings into Latin in the sixth century, the name of Syncletica became known in the west and eventually became part of the anchoritic tradition, for example, *The Ancrene Wisse*. It is also through translations of these Sayings into modern vernaculars, as well as through the recent surge of interest in all matters to do with women, that renewed attention has been focused on Syncletica and that the *Life and Regimen* in its entirety has been translated into modern renditions: French in 1972 (Bernard) and English in 1990 (Castelli) and now (1995) by the present translator.

A NOTE TO THE TRANSLATION

The Greek of Syncletica's *Life and Regimen* is in general correct and straightforward, although the style is neither subtle nor elegant. The use of moods, for example, shows little understanding of the niceties of refined Greek usage; the optative does appear occasionally and inconsistently in conditional sentences. Transitional and connective particles, especially οὖν and δέ, are used unfailingly, but unimaginatively, with little appreciation for their nuances. I have attempted to capture this banality by using "therefore," "then," and "so" far more frequently than good English usage would normally allow, but even so, the reader should not think that I have by any means accounted for them all.

Scriptural quotations are frequent throughout the text, but they are seldom exact. I have translated them as they stand in the text and have not adjusted them to any standard English translation. By doing this I hope that I have reflected the fluent and familiar way in which the author uses Scripture. In the footnotes the notation cf. before a Scriptural reference indicates that the wording in the text is not precisely that of the Septuagint or the Greek New Testament.

For those passages of the text that are also found in *The Alphabetic Collection of the Desert Fathers,* I have followed the same procedure. The translation represents what stands in the text of Syncletica's *Life and Regimen*; where that text differs from the Migne text of the *Apophthegmata Patrum* or the text in Guy's additions, the notation cf. preceding the reference in the footnotes indicates that there is a difference.

Syncletica's discourse is laden not only with Scriptural references, but with images and figurative language. For the most part the analogies between the spiritual realm and familiar elements of the material world are common ones that recur frequently in ascetic writings: for example, athletics, navigation, storms. In general these are easily understood, but at times they do present a challenge to the translator, especially when the images are mixed and inconsistent. In some passages I have resorted to the use of quotation marks to help the reader follow the shifting thought.

Another challenging feature of this text for the translator is the ascetic vocabulary. The terms used are the standard ones found in the ascetic authors in the tradition of Evagrius Ponticus, but many of these – indeed, most of them – allow for various equivalents in English. For example, ὑπερηφανία means "pride" or "arrogance"; I have used "pride" because it is the more traditional term in English for this vice. In the case of πορνεία, however, although the traditional translation is "fornication," I have not always used it, often choosing instead "sexual impurity," because "fornication" is frequently an inadequate translation of the term in context. I have tried to be consistent in translating such ascetic terms and where possible I have followed the terminology found in the most recent translations of ascetic authors.

THE LIFE & REGIMEN[1]

OF THE HOLY & BLESSED TEACHER

SYNCLETICA[2]

1

There is a need[3] for all people to live their lives with a knowledge of what is good. For if they are[4] thus trained in the practical aspects[5] [of living], they possess in life something with no liens attached[6] and, moreover, much of what is beneficial escapes the notice of those with less experience. They suffer this disadvantage as a result of the entrenchment of a perspective blurred through negligence. For often pearls of great price go unrecognised by poor men, and those inexperienced in the working of these precious gems scorn them as something small and of no value. In our own case, certainly, when we, with a soul naive and untrained, came upon a pearl in actuality, we saw it as something of no great import, judging it by appearance alone and yet, in accord with our limited knowledge, falling far short of its true nature. But when, little by little, we were taught its beauty by those close to us, a supernatural passion for what was glimpsed was engendered in us; and indeed, these glimpses fired our heart with longing.

2

But why do I mention her associates or count myself among them, as if we know and tell something special about the renowned and blessed Syncletica? For I do not think that any human being is equal to a description of her good practices. And even if someone should attempt to say something about her, he will fall immeasurably short of what is wanted, wise and learned though he may be. For just as those who wish to gaze at the sun damage their vision, so also those who try to mirror the radiance of her life fall victim to confusion of mind, dazzled, overcome, and unstrung by the magnitude of her achievements.

3

But as we investigated to the best of our ability the facts about her, we both heard from her contemporaries the superficial details of her early life and we gained some enlightenment from her deeds themselves; now we come to the writing part, storing up for ourselves the while the sustenance of salvation.[7] To tell this story in a manner worthy of her is not only beyond our powers, but difficult for the vast majority.

4

Named for the heavenly assembly [i.e. *synkletos*], Syncletica has her origins in the land of Macedonia, for when her forebears heard of the love of the Alexandrians for God and Christ, they emigrated from Macedonia to the city of the Macedonian [i.e. Alexander]. And when they arrived in the place and found the situation even better than its reputation, they joyfully made it their residence. They did not take pleasure in the large population, nor were they awestruck at the size of the buildings, but when they discovered an unmatched faith coupled with a sincere charity (cf. 1 Cor. 5: 8),[8] they made their country of adoption their second home.

5

Distinguished in lineage, the blessed Syncletica also enjoyed the other advantages that are considered desirable by worldly standards. She had, moreover, a like-minded sister and two brothers who were also esteemed for their religious way of life. The one of these passed away in childhood, but the other, on reaching his twenty-fifth year, was required to marry by his parents. When all the preparations had been made for this purpose and the legal papers were completed according to custom, however, the young man flitted away like a bird from the snare, exchanging his earthly bride for the blameless and free company of the saints.

6

But while still in her father's arms, she first began to train[9] her soul in the love of God. And she did not so much give attention to the care of her body as she did watch the urgings of her nature.

7

For she was a woman of such outstanding physical beauty that many suitors approached her in the first bloom of her youth, in part attracted by her wealth, and in part by the high rank of her parents, but in addition captivated also by the beauty of the girl herself Certainly her parents cheerfully encouraged the young woman towards marriage, promoting this plan so that through her the continuance of the family might be assured for them. Chaste and noble in mind, however, she did not cooperate at all with these plans of her parents, but as she listened to talk of a worldly marriage, she kept dreaming of a divine one, and while ignoring numbers of suitors, she reserved her approval for the heavenly Bridegroom alone.

8

One could consider her the true disciple of the blessed Thecla[10] as she followed her in the same teachings. Indeed, Christ was the one suitor of the two women, and for them both Paul was himself the "leader of the bride."[11] I also think that even their bridal chamber was not different, for the Church was their single nuptial cell. The same David too sang holy and divine canticles over them both; for with fine sounding cymbals he gladdens the souls dedicated to God, and with timbrels and ten-stringed psalteries he sends up his perfect song (Ps

150: 4, 5; Ps 92: 4 (LXX 91: 4). And for these holy wedding rites Miriam leads in the dancers with the words: Let us sing to the Lord for he is gloriously triumphant (Ex 15: 1); and to those sharing the delicacies of the divine banquet, Taste and see that the Lord is good (Ps 34: 9 (LXX 33: 9). And a single cloth they had for their wedding robes, All who were baptised into Christ clothed themselves with Christ (Gal 3: 27). They had, therefore, a love for Christ of the same kind, for they were deemed worthy of the same gifts, but, even more, they contended with the same struggles. The acts of witness of the blessed Thecla are known to all–how through fire and wild beasts she struggled valiantly; and I do not think that Syncletica's virtuous sufferings and exertions go unnoticed by the crowd. But if one Saviour was the object of their longing, then necessarily one Enemy was also their adversary. And, I fancy, Thecla's sufferings were milder, for the evil of the Enemy was diminished since he attacked her from without. But in Syncletica's case, he demonstrates his more piercing brand of evil by disturbing her from within through her own contrary and destructive thoughts.

9

The weave of an embroidered garment did not beguile her eye, nor the various hues of precious stones; the cymbal did not delude her hearing nor was the flute able to slacken the tenor of her soul. The tears of her parents did not weaken her resolve nor did any other advice from her relatives; on the contrary, she adamantly maintained her intention and did not change her resolution. Moreover, by closing her senses as if they were windows, she continued to converse in solitude with her bridegroom, referring to the following passage: I belong to my beloved and my beloved belongs to me (cf. Song 2: 16). If conversations of a questionable and unedifying nature were taking place, she avoided them, retreating to the inner treasure chambers of her soul; but where enlightened and helpful counsels were being offered, she concentrated her whole mind on receiving what was being said.

10

Neither did she neglect the treatment that brings salvation for the body. She held fasting so dear that no one of her associates equalled her, for she considered this practice a safeguard and foundation for the other virtues. But when under force of circumstances she took nourishment according to the normal schedule,[12] she experienced a reaction opposite to that of people accustomed to eating: her face grew pale, the weight of her body diminished, for when one does something against the grain, what is done likewise changes character. Whatever the beginning may be, the consequences are entirely consistent. And so, for those to whom eating brings both pleasure and profit, the weight of the body thrives, but for those for whom the opposite situation exists, the flesh becomes malnourished and wasted–the sick bear witness to what I say. Certainly this blessed woman achieved good health for her soul while trying to control her body, for she was acting according to the Apostle when he says: As our outer person perishes, so our inner person is being renewed (cf. 2 Cor 4: 16). In this way, then, she continued her struggle without generally attracting attention.

11

But when her parents came to the end of life, Syncletica was inspired by divine will to greater heights; taking her sister with her (for her sister was blind), she left her paternal home. She went to a tomb of a relative of hers which stood at a distance from the city.[13] After selling all the property left to her and distributing it to the poor, she summoned one of the priests and cut off her own hair. At that moment she laid aside all "worldly glory," for women customarily refer to their hair as their "glory."[14] This act was a sign that her soul had become unadorned[15] and pure. And so, then, for the first time, she was deemed worthy of the title "virgin."

12

After distributing all her substance to the poor, she said: "I have been judged worthy of a great title. What worthy return shall I make to the giver? I do not have anything. If in the outside world, for the sake of a transitory distinction, people throw away their whole substance, how much more necessary is it for me who have been granted so great a grace to offer my body along with what are regarded as possessions? But why do I talk about giving possessions or body when all that is belongs to him? *For the Lord's is the earth and its fullness* (Ps 24: 1 (LXX 23: 1). Once she had *clothed herself with humility* (cf. 1 Pet 5: 5) by means of these words, she entered upon a solitary life.

13

Even in her father's house, however, she was reasonably well practiced in austerities and was already making progress in virtue when she entered upon this crucial stage of her course. Those people, you see, who come to this divine mystery without training and reflection do not find[16] what they seek, since they have not first examined what is needed in detail. But just as those contemplating a journey first think about their provisions, so she also prepared herself over time with austerities and generously provided herself with the necessities for her journey to the heights. For, by arranging in advance what she needed for the construction of her building, she succeeded in making her tower very sturdy (cf. Lk 14: 28). Now the construction of buildings is traditionally carried out with materials from without, but she went about it in the opposite way; she did not gather all her building materials from without, but rather she emptied herself of what was within. For by giving her possessions to the poor, by relinquishing anger and vindictiveness, and by driving away envy and ambition, she built her house on rock, its tower visible from afar and its structure storm proof (cf. Mt 7: 24).

14

And why do I go on at length? In her beginnings she surpassed even those who were accustomed to the solitary life. Just as the most naturally gifted children, while still learning their letters, compete with those who are older and have spent more time with their teachers, so also this woman, fervent in spirit (cf. Rom 12:11), sprinted past all other women.

15

We cannot speak, then, of her actual ascetic life, since she did not allow anyone to be an observer of this. Nor did she wish her associates to be "heralds" of her heroic virtues. For she did not so much think about doing good as she did about keeping her good works private and secret. She acted in this way not because she was pressured by envy, but because she was supported by divine grace. For she kept in mind that saying of the Lord to the effect: *if your right hand does something, let your left hand not know it* (cf. Mt 6: 3). And thus, in private, she fulfilled the demands of her calling.

16

From her earliest years right up to her maturity she not only avoided encounters with any male, but she also often rejected females for two reasons: to avoid publicity because of the severity of her asceticism and to avoid distraction from virtue because of her physical needs.

17

Thus, therefore, she kept careful watch over the first impulses of her soul, not allowing them to be led astray by physical passions. And, like a tree gone wild, she was pruned of her unfruitful branches, her superfluous growth. Through fasting and prayer she trimmed the thorny offshoots of her thought. And if anyone of these managed to grow a little, she applied to it various kinds of penalties, mistreating her body with all sorts of austerities. She not only made do with a minimum amount of bread, but also with a very small amount of water.

18

When the Enemy's campaign was being directed against her, first of all through prayer she used to call upon her Master to join in the battle, for she was not strong enough to quell the onslaught of the lion (cf. 1 Pet 5: 8) by asceticism alone. And at the instant of her supplication, the Lord was at her side and the Enemy was in flight. But often too her Foe would linger for battle and the Lord would not ward off the Fiend, by this very means intending to increase the training of her virtuous soul. At this increase, as it were, of gifts, she was empowered all the more for victory against the Foe. In mortifying herself she was content not just with a reduced diet, but she also tried to seal herself off from pleasurable habits. She used to eat bran bread; often she took no water at all; she also used to sleep on the ground for brief periods at a time.[17] And so, as long as the battle was in progress, she would wield such weapons, clad in prayer for her armour and breastplate, with helmet crafted from faith, hope, and love (cf. Eph 6: 16–18). But faith took precedence over all in strengthening her total defences.[18] Almsgiving was also practised, if not in actuality, certainly, then, in intent.

19

Moreover, when the Enemy was sustaining defeat because of these practices, she also used to mitigate the severity of her asceticism. And this she used to do so that the parts of her body might not become totally debilitated – for physical collapse was a sign of defeat. After all, once his weapons are damaged, what hope does a soldier have for war? Some, to be sure, would inflict the fatal blow on themselves by spending themselves in fasting without moderation or judgement. And once they were at the mercy, so to speak, of the Adversary, they brought about their own destruction. She, however, did not act in this way, but did everything with discernment and so continued to fight valiantly against the Foe through prayers and asceticism. She would take care of her body when her ship, so to speak, was in calm waters. In actual fact, those who sail ships go without food when stormy weather and high seas overtake them, while they apply all their skill to the danger before their eyes. But when they succeed in surviving, then they take thought for a second kind of salvation. Nor is all their time spent on the surging sea, but they welcome the briefest calm spell as a rest from their labours. But even so they neither pass their time free from care nor sink into deep sleep indeed, since, with their experience of the past, they take thought for the future. For, even if the storm has abated, still the sea has not lost its power; and if the second crisis has passed, nevertheless the third lies ahead. Even if what happened is behind them, still what caused it is at hand. So then, in the present case too, even if the spirit of lust has been banished, still, nevertheless, the one who arouses it is not far off. It is necessary, therefore, to pray unceasingly (cf. 1 Thess 5: 17) because of the instability of the sea and the bitter malice of the Enemy. The blessed Syncletica, therefore, with her accurate apprehension of the ever-present tempests in life and her expectations of gusts of winds, continued steering her own little boat attentively with reverence toward God. She did in fact bring it undamaged by storms to safe harbour, having placed her faith in God as her surest anchor.[19]

20

Her life, therefore, was apostolic, constrained by faith and holy poverty,[20] yet still, to be sure, radiant with love and humility. Her conduct was the fulfillment of the saving word. *For you shall tread upon asp and viper* (cf. Ps 91: 13; LXX 90: 13) *and on all the power of the enemy* (Lk 10: 19). Fittingly she heard this message: *Well done, good and faithful servant; you were faithful in a few matters, I shall set you up over many* (cf. Mt 25: 21). Even though this message refers to gifts, in this instance nevertheless it should be interpreted in the following way: "Because you were victorious in the war of the flesh, you will also carry off a trophy in the war of the spirit, under the protection of my shield. Let those *principalities and powers* (cf. Eph 6: 12) spoken of by my servant Paul know the greatness of your faith; for, since you have vanquished the opposing forces, you will encounter even stronger ones."

21

Thus, then, going apart on her own, she continued perfecting her good works. And as time progressed and her virtues were blossoming, the sweet scent (2 Cor 2: 15) of her widely renowned austerities spread to many, for, Scripture says, (cf. Mt 10: 26). Even on his own God knows how to proclaim those who love him for the correction of those who listen. At that time, therefore, some women began to come by in their wish for something better and to make appeals for their edification. Since, in fact, they profited through their discussions in exchanging information about Syncletica's life, they began to come more and more often in their desire to be helped. According to their customary procedure they would put questions to her, saying: "How must one be saved?" And with a deep groan and a flood of tears, she would withdraw into herself and would again observe silence as if her tears were answer enough. But the women, acting as a group, would force her to speak of the great deeds of God. Actually they were stunned and amazed just by the sight of her. Again they would call upon her to speak. And under great pressure, after quite a long time spent in deepest silence, the blessed woman would recite in a low voice that passage from Scripture: *Do no violence to a poor man, for he is needy* (Prov 22: 22). The women present received this response gladly as if they had tasted of honey and honeycomb, and continued their questioning even more. And from then on they used to challenge her through scriptural passages, for they would say to her: *"You received a gift, give a gift"* (cf. Mt 10: 8). Or they might say:[21] *"See to it that you do not pay instead of the servant for the hidden talent"* (cf. Mt 25: 30). But she would say to them: "Why do you fantasise in this way about a sinner like me as if I were doing or saying something worthwhile? We have a common teacher–the Lord; we draw spiritual water from the same well and we suck our milk from the same breasts–the Old and the New Testaments." But they would say to her: "We also know that we have one source of instruction – Scripture – and the same teacher. But you have made progress in virtues by your ever-wakeful zeal; those who are in possession of what is good, since they are better able, must also help those who are weaker. And indeed our common teacher commands this." And on hearing these words, the blessed woman used to weep, like babes at the breast. But the women gathered there put aside their questioning once more and urged her to stop weeping. And when she had grown calm, there was again a long period of silence and again they began to encourage her. Since she was deeply moved and knew, moreover, that what she had said did not bring praise for herself but rather sowed helpful ideas among those present, she began to speak to them in the following vein.

22

"My children, all of us – male and female – know about being saved, but through our own negligence we stray from the path of salvation.[22] First of all we must observe the precepts known through the grace of the Lord, and these are: You shall love the Lord your God with your whole soul, and your neighbour as yourself (cf. Mt 22: 37, 39). In these precepts the first principle of the Law is preserved, and it is on this Law that the fullness of grace depends. The expression of the principle is brief indeed, but its importance in this matter is great and unlimited, for all advice to help the soul depends on these precepts. Paul also bears witness to this when he says that the end of law is love (cf. Rom 13: 10; 1 Tim 1: 5). Whatever people say by the grace of the Spirit, therefore, that is useful springs from love and ends in it. Salvation, then, is exactly this – the two-fold love of God and of our neighbour.

23

"And this thought that also arises from the same love should be added: each one[23] of us knows what it is to strive for greater things."

But the women were puzzled at her statement and again they questioned her. And so she spoke to them as follows. "You are not unaware of the parable in the gospel about the hundred-fold, sixty-fold, and thirty-fold return (Mt 13: 8). The hundred-fold refers to our calling; the sixty-fold to the ranks of the continent; and the thirty-fold to the ranks of those who live chastely.[24] It is a good thing to move from the thirty-fold category to the sixty-fold, for it is good to advance from the small to the greater, but to descend from the greater to the smaller is dangerous. For the person who has once given assent to what is less than good is unable to stand firm even in little matters, but is carried off, so to speak, into the pit of destruction. Some women, certainly, although professing virginity, are led astray by the reasoning of a weak mind and *invent pretexts for their sins* (cf. Ps 141: 4; LXX 140: 4). For they say to themselves (or rather, to the Devil): 'If we live chastely'[25] (or rather, foolishly), we will be considered worthy at least of the thirty-fold return.' They also say, 'The whole of the Old Testament has supported procreation.' It should be recognised, therefore, that this view is the Enemy's, for someone who is drawn from the greater to the lesser is being 'thrown' by the Adversary. For the person who does this is judged like a soldier who deserts; he is not awarded pardon because he left for a less strenuous campaign, but he has received punishment because he ran away. As I said earlier, it is, therefore, necessary to advance from the lesser to the greater. And this, too, the Apostle teaches: *Forgetting what lies behind, one must strive after what lies ahead* (cf. Phil 3: 13). Those who are winning control of the hundred-fold return must keep repeating this for themselves and not set a limit on the amount of return, for Scripture says: If you have done what was ordered, say 'We are useless servants' (cf. Lk 17: 10).

24

"Therefore, we who have taken up this calling must practise chastity to the utmost. Actually, even among secular women chastity is regarded as worth cultivating, but immorality also flourishes among them because they sin through all their other senses. For example, they allow their eyes to wander at random and they laugh inappropriately.[26] But let us firmly reject these practices also and move ever onwards and upwards in our virtues; let us remove from our sight empty fantasy. For Scripture does say: *Let your eyes look straight ahead* (cf. Prov 4: 25). It bids us to check our tongue also from such sins, since it is not right for the instrument of hymns to express shameful words; not only should speaking them be avoided, but even hearing them.

25

"It is impossible, however, to observe these rules if we frequently make public excursions. For through our senses, even if we are unwilling, 'thieves' enter. How indeed can a house not be blackened when smoke from outside is wafting about and the windows are open?[27] It is imperative, therefore, that sallies out into the market-place be avoided. If we consider it troublesome and oppressive to see our brothers and parents naked, how much more harmful it will be for us to view on the streets people indecently clad and, even worse, speaking licentious words? For it is from these experiences that disgusting and virulent images arise.

26

"When, moreover, we do confine ourselves to our houses, not even there should we be careless, but should maintain our vigilance, for it has been written: *Stay awake!* (Mt 24: 42). The more we secure ourselves in chastity, the more we are plied with galling thoughts; as Scripture says: *The one who increases his knowledge increases his sorrow* (cf. Eccl 1: 18). For the more athletes make progress, the more they are matched with stronger opponents.[28] Consider how much you have advanced, and you will not underestimate the present situation.[29] Were you victorious over actual physical sexual impurity?[30] Then the Enemy will inflict it upon you through the senses. And when you protect yourself from this too, he continues to lurk in the crannies of the mind, stirring up a battle of the spirit for you. Even for women who live as solitaries he conjures up handsome faces and old relationships. It is essential, therefore, not to give your assent to these fantasies, for it has been written: *If the spirit of the ruler rise up against you, do not yield your place* (Eccl 10: 4). Giving your assent to these fantasies, moreover, is equivalent to sexual impurity in the world; Scripture says: *But for those in power a powerful testing will be imposed* (Wis 6: 8). The struggle against the spirit of sexual impurity, therefore, is a major one, since it is the chief among the Enemy's evils directed to the destruction of the soul. This is what blessed Job is suggesting when he referred to the Devil as the one who has power in the navel of his belly (cf. Job 40: 16).[31]

27

"With many and varied stratagems, therefore, the Devil applies the goad of sexual impurity to people who love Christ. To be sure, the Malevolent One has often transformed even sisterly love into his own brand of evil. He has actually tripped up, through their attachment to their sisters, virgins who have fled from marriage and all worldly illusion; and monks too he has wounded, even those in flight from every kind of sexual impurity whatever, but them also he has deceived by means of their religious relationships. For this is the task of the Enemy: to promote his own plans unobserved, in a disguise of some kind. He puts out a scrap of food and underneath it he places a snare. I think that the Lord too is speaking about this: They come to you in sheep's clothing, but within they are ravenous wolves (Mt 7: 15).

28

"What, then, are we to do against this danger? *Let us become cunning as serpents and innocent as doves* (cf. Mt 10: 16), pitting against his snare all our intellectual resources. For the advice *Be cunning as serpents* has been given so that we may not fail to notice the onslaughts of the Devil; for *like* very quickly earns recognition from *like*. Innocence of the dove indicates purity of action.[32] Every good deed, then, will be a move away from something worse. But how are we to escape what we do not know? Well, we must take stock of the cleverness of the Enemy and be on guard against his evil devices. For Scripture speaks of *the one who prowls around, looking for someone to devour* (cf. 1 Pet 5: 8). And it says also, *His food is choice* (Hab 1: 16). At all times, therefore, there is a need for vigilance; for he wages war through external acts and wins victories through internal thoughts. And he accomplishes more through internal thoughts, for, unseen, he keeps attacking by night and day.

29

"Well, what do we need for the present conflict? Obviously, austere asceticism and pure prayer. These, however, provide a general protection against all destructive thought, but it is necessary to employ some particular mental devices to ward off from ourselves the infection of the soul that threatens at the moment and to counter base thoughts with their opposites as they are attacking. For example, if in the crannies of the mind there should appear a vision of a beautiful apparition, it should be opposed instantly by one's rational faculty. One should mentally gouge out the eyes of the image, and tear the flesh from its cheeks, and slash off the lips too–then one should look at the ugly framework of the bare bones! then one should view with scorn what was the object of desire! For thus the mind would have the strength to retreat from a foolish deception. The love object was nothing but blood mixed with phlegm, a mixture that for living creatures requires a covering. In this way, then, also through such mental processes it is possible to frighten off the foul evil. Just as it is appropriate to drive out a nail with a nail, so it is appropriate to drive out a demon.[33] And still further, one should imagine over the entire body of the object of lust foul-smelling and festering sores, and to see it with the inner eye, to put it briefly, as something like a corpse or even to see oneself as a corpse. And most important of all is control over the belly, for thus is possible also control over the pleasures beneath the belly."

30

There was in progress, therefore, a godly symposium of the women present;[34] for they were celebrating from the cups of wisdom–and pouring the divine draught and water[35] was the blessed Syncletica. And each one of the women was receiving what she wanted. One of those gathered there put a question to her, saying: "Is voluntary poverty[36] a perfect good?"

And Syncletica answered: "It is certainly a good for those women who are able to endure it. For the women who persevere in this condition have suffering in the flesh, but peace in the soul. For just as heavy clothing is washed and bleached by treading and vigorous wringing, so also the strong soul is strengthened to a greater degree through voluntary poverty.[37] But those with a weaker disposition have the opposite experience to the first women. Indeed, when they are rubbed a little, they disintegrate like torn garments, not lasting through the wash with their virtue. And, although the fuller may be the same, the outcome for the clothes is different; some are torn and perished while another is bleached and renewed.[38] One could say, then, that, for the courageous[39] mind, voluntary poverty is a good to be treasured, for it is truly a curb to committing sins.

31

"But first it is essential to be trained in austerities; I mean by fasting, by sleeping on the ground and by other austerities in turn, and thus to acquire this virtue. For those who have not proceeded in this fashion, but who have suddenly rushed into rejecting their possessions are generally seized with regret.

32

"For possessions are the 'tools' of a life devoted to pleasure. Take away first the 'trade' (i.e., gluttony and soft living), and you will also be able easily to dispense with its material aspect represented by your possessions; for it is difficult, in my opinion, if the 'trade' is going on, for the 'tools' to be absent. For if a woman has not given up the first, how will she be able to reject the second? For this reason even the Saviour in his conversation with the rich man does not suddenly suggest to him the casting aside of his possessions, but asks him whether he has fulfilled the precepts of the Law. Taking on the role of the true teacher, moreover, the Lord asks: 'Have you learned your letters? Have you understood the syllables? and have you thoroughly grasped the vocabulary? Advance, then, to the actual reading.' (That is, *Come, sell your goods, and then follow me* [cf. Mt 19: 21]. I imagine that the Lord would not have directed him to voluntary poverty if he had not given assurance that he had fulfilled the commandments. For how would he have been able to advance to 'reading' without knowing the value of the 'syllables'?

33

"And so, voluntary poverty is a good for those who have been in the habit of good practices. For once they have cast off all superfluous possessions, they bring to the Lord the sign of their commitment as they sing in purity that inspired passage that says: *Our eyes look to you in hope; and you give food in due season to those that love you* (cf. Ps 145: 15; LXX 144: 15).

34

"In other ways too those who practise poverty gain a great benefit; for, by not focusing their mind on treasure here on earth, they are putting on the kingdom of heaven and clearly fulfilling the declaration of the hymnist David which says: *I became beast-like in your presence* (Ps 73: 22; LXX 72: 22). For just as domestic animals in the performance of their particular tasks are satisfied only with the nourishment needed to maintain life, so also those who practise poverty consider the use of silver worthless and they do their manual work in return for their daily nourishment alone. These people possess the foundation of faith; for them was spoken by the Lord the passage about not taking thought for the morrow (Mt 6: 34) *and the birds of the sky do not sow, nor do they reap . . . and the Father in heaven nourishes them* (cf. Mt 6: 26). In these words they have found encouragement (for God was the one who said them) and with confidence they acclaim that passage from Scripture: *I believed; therefore I spoke* (Ps 116: 10; LXX 115: 1).

35

"The Enemy, moreover, is more soundly vanquished in the case of those who live without possessions; for he lacks the means to do harm, since the majority of our griefs and trials originate in the removal of possessions. What course of action does he have against those without possessions? None! Can he burn their estates? Impossible! Destroy their livestock? They do not even have any! Lay hands on their dear ones? To these too they long ago said good-bye. And so voluntary poverty is a powerful retribution against the Enemy as well as a precious treasure for the soul.

36

"Just as this poverty, then, is admirable and important for virtue, so is love of money contemptible and culpable for evil. And truly about this vice the inspired Paul said that it was the cause of all evils (cf. 1 Tim 6: 10). Lust for wealth, perjury, theft, robbery, sexual impurity, envy, hatred of brethren, war, idolatry, covetousness (and the offshoots of these: hypocrisy, flattery, ridicule) – of all these vices, then, the cause is declared to be love of money. Rightly, therefore, the Apostle named it the mother of all evils. But not only does God exact punishment for these vices, but they also bring about their own destruction out of their very nature. For in bringing evil that is insatiable they do not have a limit to their goal, and so their wound is incurable. The one who has nothing desires little, and on acquiring this little, reaches for more. One has a hundred gold coins and longs for a thousand, and after acquiring these, raises his sights ad infinitum. And so, unable to establish their limit, they continually lament their poverty. Also, love of money always brings with it envy. And this also destroys first the person possessed by it. For just as the viper on its birth first destroys its own mother before it harms others,[40] so also envy wastes the one possessed by it before it spreads to those around it.

37

"It would be a great advantage if, in our search for genuine wealth, we could endure as many tribulations as those hopelessly damaging ones that 'hunters' of empty worldliness encounter. They suffer shipwrecks, they consort with pirates, on land they fall among thieves;

furthermore, they undergo storms and violent winds, and often, when they are prospering, they say they are paupers because of envious people. We, however, take no such risks for the sake of genuine profit. But if ever we women[41] do experience some little gain, we puff ourselves up, pointing it out to people. In addition we often fail to include in our account what really happened, and so immediately we are robbed by the Enemy even of the spark of good we thought we possessed. And those people too, while making their many profits, keep going after more; they count as nothing what they already have, and keep reaching out after what they do not have. We, however, do not want to possess anything, even though we possess nothing of what was being sought;[42] we call ourselves rich even while plagued by extreme poverty. It is good, therefore, for someone who is prospering not to announce it to anyone, for such people will be punished more; what they think they possess will be taken from them (cf. Lk 8: 18).

38

"We must make every effort, then, to keep our 'gain' hidden. Those who are describing their own successes should also try to mention the weaknesses that go with them. But if they conceal these weaknesses in order not to be reproached by their listeners, they should far rather be keeping watch on them as factors alienating them from God. Certainly those who live in virtue act in the opposite way; they describe their small lapses along with some extras which they did not commit, thus rejecting the good esteem of people while concealing their good acts for the safety of their soul. For as a treasure is spent once it has been revealed, so virtue also vanishes once it is known and made public. Just as wax melts in the presence of fire, so also does the soul disintegrate in the face of praises and lose its vigour.[43]

39

"And again the opposite of this also holds true; for if heat has melted the wax, then cold will bring about its hardening. And if praise removes the vigour of the soul, then assuredly censure and insult lead the soul to heights of virtue. *Rejoice,* Scripture says, *and be glad when people speak against you every kind of lie* (cf.Mt 5: 11, 12). Elsewhere it says, *By affliction you extend me* (cf. Ps 4: 1; LXX 4: 2). And again, *My soul has awaited rebuke and humiliation* (LXX Ps 68: 21). There are countless other such good passages to be seen in Holy Scripture which are of benefit to the soul.

40

"There is a sadness that is helpful and a sadness that is destructive. It is a function of the useful sorrow, then, to lament about one's own sins as well as the ignorance of one's neighbours, but also to avoid falling away from one's purpose and to achieve the goal of goodness. These concerns, therefore, are the signs of a sorrow that is legitimate and good. There is also another kind of sorrow, prompted by the Enemy, which knows how to merge with the first kind. For he himself imposes a sorrow, completely irrational, which has also been called by some *akedia*.[44] This spirit, therefore, must be driven off especially by prayer and psalmody.[45]

41

"While we are preoccupied with our virtuous concerns, we should not think that anyone in life is free from care. For Scripture says: *Every head [is destined] for pain, and every heart for sadness* (Isa 1: 5). In a single phrase the Holy Spirit has described both the monastic life and the secular. For by *the pain of the head* he signifies the monastic way of life. The head, after all, is the governing factor, for since the eyes of the wise man are in his head, as Scripture says (Eccl 2: 14), then, I think, discernment resides in it. It says *pain,* furthermore, because every sprig of virtue grows straight as a result of pains.[46] And by sadness in the heart it has revealed the unstable and troublesome character [of secular life]. For some call the heart the seat of anger and sadness. When they are not honoured, they are sad; when they yearn for what belongs to another, they pine away; when they are poor, they feel distressed; when rich, they become obsessed, unable to sleep for watching over their possessions.

42

"Let us women[47] not be misled by the thought that those in the world are without cares. For perhaps in comparison they struggle more than we do. For towards women generally there is great hostility in the world. They bear children with difficulty and risk, and they suffer patiently through nursing, and they share illnesses with their sick children – and these things they endure without having any limit to their travail. For either the children they bear are maimed in body, or, brought up in perversity, they treacherously murder their parents. Since we women know these facts, therefore, let us not be deluded by the Enemy that their life is easy and carefree. For in giving birth women die in labour; and yet, in failing to give birth, they waste away under reproaches that they are barren and unfruitful.[48]

43

"I am telling you these things to safeguard you from the Adversary. What is being said, however, is not suitable for all, but only for those who choose the monastic life. For just as one diet is not suitable for all animals, so the same instruction is not appropriate for all people. As Scripture says: *one should not put new wine into old wineskins* (Mt 9: 17). Those who find satisfaction in contemplation and spiritual enlightenment [*gnosis*] are nourished in one way, while those who have a taste for asceticism and its practical application [*praktike*][49] are nourished in another way, and similarly those in the world who practise good works to the best of their ability. For just as some living creatures are land animals, some are water animals, and some winged, so also are human beings; some people choose the middle road (as land animals do), some look to the heights (as birds do), and others (like fish) are concealed in the waters of their sins. Scripture says: *I came into the depths of the sea, and a storm engulfed me* (Ps 69: 2; LXX 68: 3). And such is the nature of living creatures. But since we women[50] have grown wings like eagles,[51] let us soar to the higher places, and let us trample underfoot the lion and the dragon (cf. LXX Ps 90: 13); and let us now rule over the one who once ruled over us. And this we shall do if we offer to the Saviour our whole mind.

44

"But as we rise toward the high places, that Enemy also strives to entangle us in his own snares. And why is it remarkable that we women[52] have adversaries as we strive for the good, when indeed they are grudging even in matters of little account? Certainly they do not allow people to take treasures buried beneath the earth; if, then, they offer opposition even to earthbound daydreams, how much more grudging they will be in respect to the kingdom of Heaven!

45

"We must, therefore, arm ourselves against them in every way, for they attack indeed from without and they are no less active from within.[53] Like a ship our soul is sometimes engulfed by the waves without and is sometimes swamped by the bilge-water within. Certainly we too sometimes perish through sins committed externally, but we sometimes are destroyed by thoughts within us. And so we must guard against onslaughts of spirits from outside us, and bail out impurities of thoughts inside us;[54] and we must always be vigilant with regard to our thoughts, for they are a constant threat to us. Against the storm waves outside salvation often comes from ships nearby when the sailors cry out for help; but bilge-waters overflow and frequently kill the seamen, often when they are asleep and the sea is calm.

46

"Consequently, the mind must become painstakingly diligent with respect to its thoughts. For when the Enemy wants to destroy the soul as he would a building, he engineers its collapse from the foundations, or he begins from the roof and topples the whole structure; or, he goes in through the windows, ties up the master of the house first and thus wins control of everything. 'Foundation', then, signifies good works, 'roof' faith, and 'windows' the senses. And through all of them the Enemy wages war. And so the person wishing to be saved must be very watchful. We do not have here something to be careless about;[55] for Scripture says: *Let the one standing firm take care lest he fall* (cf. 1 Cor. 10: 12).

47

"We are sailing in uncertainty. For our life is a sea, as has been said by the holy psalmist David (cf Ps 69: 2; LXX 68: 3). But some parts of the sea are full of reefs and some full also of monsters, but some too are calm. We seem to be sailing in the calm part of the sea while secular people sail in the dangerous parts. We also sail during the day, navigating by the sun of righteousness (Mal 4: 2), while they sail by night, swept along by ignorance. It often happens, however, that the secular person has saved his ship in the midst of storm and darkness by crying out and staying awake; we, on the other hand, have drowned in calm waters through carelessness in letting go of the rudder of righteousness.

48

"Let the one standing firm, therefore, *take care lest he fall* (cf. 1 Cor 10: 12). For the one who has fallen has a single thought – that of standing up again; but the one who is standing firm should be on his guard so as not to fall. Actually, 'falls' are of different sorts. Those who have fallen have, to be sure, lost their footing; but as they lie there, they have not suffered any harm. And the one who has kept his footing should not judge inferior the one who has fallen, but should fear for himself, lest he fall and perish, and go to a deeper pit. For probably, since his cry for help will be muffled by the depth of the pit, he will not be able to ask for help. For the just person says: *Let not the abyss swallow me up nor let the pit close its mouth over me* (Ps 69: 15; LXX 68: 16). The first mortal who fell remained down. Watch out for yourself lest you fall and also become a morsel for wild beasts. The one who has fallen does not make safe his door; do not allow yourself to be caught napping on any account, but always sing out that inspired message that says: *Lighten my eyes, lest I sleep unto death* (Ps 13: 3; LXX 12: 4). And stay awake without ceasing because of *the roaring lion* (cf. Pet 5: 8).

49

"These words are useful against feeling superior. The one who has fallen will be saved by conversion and weeping. You, [O sister],[56] who are still on your feet, look to yourself. For two fears threaten you: either that you will return to your old ways because the Enemy has attacked you through your negligence, or that you will be tripped while on course. Our Enemy the Devil either draws us to himself from behind when he sees our soul sluggish and slothful, or through pride he attacks subtly and secretly a soul that considers itself zealous and diligent in discipline – thus he destroys the soul utterly. This weapon [i.e., discipline] is the ultimate and chief of all evils! With it, the Devil has been himself defeated and through it, he tries to overthrow the strongest of people. Just as the most formidable of warriors introduces the strongest blade of all if their opponents are still holding out after the use of lighter weapons, so also the Devil, after first using his 'snares,' then uses his ultimate 'sword' pride. But what were his first 'snares'? Obviously, gluttony, love of pleasure, sexual impurity. For these spirits in particular occur together in the younger age groups. And there follow on these love of money, covetousness, and the like. Therefore, when the unhappy soul prevails over these passions, when it gains control of the belly, when it transcends even sexual impurity with holiness, when it scorns money, the Malevolent One, confounded on all sides, instigates in the soul an irregular impulse. He puffs the soul up so that it is inappropriately conceited in relation to its sisters. Grievous and deadly is this poison of the Enemy! By means of it, he has suddenly blinded and cast down many. For he suggests to the soul a thought that is false and deadly; it imagines that it has grasped matters that are incomprehensible to the majority and that it is superior in fasting. And he suggests to the soul a host of heroic deeds; he seduces it into forgetting all its sins to make it feel superior in comparison with its associates. He steals from its mind the memory of its mistakes; he does not do this for the soul's benefit, but so that it will not be able to speak that healing utterance: *Against you alone did I sin; have mercy on me* (cf. Ps 51: 4, 1; LXX 50: 6 and 3). Nor indeed will he allow the soul to say: *I will give praise to you, Lord, with all my heart* (Ps 22: 2; LXX 110: 1). But just as the Devil himself said in his mind: I shall go up and place my throne [above the stars] (Isa 14: 13), so he deludes this person with positions of command and high offices, and again with teaching posts and displays of healing. Thus deceived, then, the soul perishes and is destroyed, smitten with a wound hard to heal.

50

"What must one do, then, when such thoughts are present? Without ceasing one must meditate upon that inspired word which the blessed

David proclaimed when he said: *but I am a worm and not a human being* (Ps 22: 6; LXX 21: 7). And in another passage Scripture says: *but I am earth and ashes* (Gen 18: 27). And also, to be sure, one should listen to that passage of Isaiah, the one which says: *All human righteousness is like a filthy rag* (cf. Isa 64: 6; LXX 64: 5). If these thoughts come to the mind of a woman leading an anchorite's life, she must enter a community; and she must be forced to eat even twice a day if, at least, she is caught up in this illness through an excess of discipline. And she should be censured by her associates and rebuked; yes, she should be censured as vigorously as someone who is doing nothing important. She should also perform every act of service. And, further, the most renowned lives of the Saints should be presented for comment. The women of the community, too, should try to extend their austerities for a few days so that she may judge herself inferior once she has seen the extent of their virtues.

51

"But another evil precedes this malady: disobedience. And thus, by means of the opposing virtue of obedience, it is possible to cleanse the festering cancer of the soul, for *obedience*, Scripture says, *is better than sacrifice* (cf. 1 Sam 15: 22; LXX 1 Kgs 15: 22).

52

"It is necessary, therefore, to put a stop to the burgeoning of vainglory at the right moment, but also again at the right moment to give praise and to express admiration. For if the soul has been found negligent and slothful, and even paralysed in the growth of goodness, it is appropriate to give it praise. And if this soul does some small good, one should admire it and flatter it. Its serious and inhuman faults, however, should be spoken of as very slight and of no account. For in his desire to overturn everything, the devil tries to conceal previous sins in the case of zealous and ascetic persons because he wants to increase their pride. But in the case of newly converted and less firmly committed souls, he places all their sins before their eyes. To such a soul he suggests: 'Since you have committed sexual impurities, what forgiveness will there be?' And to another he says: 'Since you have been so greedy, you cannot obtain salvation.' Souls, then, that have been thus shaken should be comforted in the following way – in fact, it is essential to speak to them in this way – 'Rahab was a prostitute, but she was saved through faith (cf. Heb 11: 31); Paul was a persecutor, but he became a chosen instrument (Acts 9: 15); Matthew was a tax collector, but no one is ignorant of the grace granted him (cf. Mt 9: 9); and the thief stole and murdered, but he was the first to open the door of Paradise (cf. Lk 23: 43). Keeping these people in mind, therefore, do not give up hope for your own soul.'

53

"When you have found these appropriate treatments for such women, you must also apply the same therapy to those held in thrall by pride. For you should say to such a woman: 'Why are you conceited? for not eating meat? Others do not even look at fish. Even if you do not drink wine, notice how others do not eat so much as an olive. Do you fast until late in the day? Well, other women continue without food through two and three days. Do you think it is something noteworthy that you do not bathe? Many people have not indulged at all in this even during a bodily illness. Do you admire yourself because you sleep on a mat? and with goat's hair bedding? Well, other women sleep on the ground all the time. But even if you were to do this, it is nothing remarkable; some people even lie on stones to keep from meeting their physical needs with pleasure, and others, too, suspend themselves for the whole night. But even if you were to do all these things, and were successfully practising the most extreme asceticism, do not make too much of it! For demons have in fact done and are doing more ascetic acts than yours. They do not eat, nor drink, nor sleep. They also spend their lives in a desert – in case you think that you are doing something great by living in a cave.'

54

"In this way it is also possible for the two opposing maladies to be healed by similar thought therapies: I mean despair and pride. For just as a fire that is blown on vigorously is scattered, snuffed out and dies unless it gets air again, so also virtue is dissipated by pride if it exercises great severity in discipline. And again, good perishes as a result of negligence whenever we fail to bestir ourselves at the breath of the Holy Spirit. A sharp knife is easily broken by a stone, and a rigid discipline soon dissolves under the influence of pride. It is appropriate, then, for the soul on all sides to be made secure, and for the keenest discipline to take refuge in shady spots when scorched by the heat of pride. Sometimes it is also appropriate to prune what is superfluous so that the root may better flourish.

55

"Also the person in the grip of despair must be forced to move ahead by the aforementioned thought therapies, for in fact the soul is bound firmly to the earth. The best farmers, indeed, water abundantly whenever they see a plant that is stunted and weak, and they consider it very worthwhile to make it grown. But, on the other hand, whenever they see premature growth in a plant, they personally cut away what is superfluous, for this growth usually withers quickly. And for some sick people doctors prescribe nourishment freely and encourage them to walk, but others they keep confined and without food for a long time.[57]

56

"Obviously. then. the greatest among evils is pride; its opposite virtue (i.e. humility) points to this conclusion. It is difficult for anyone to acquire humility; for, unless one is beyond all vainglory, one will not be able to obtain this treasure. But so great a virtue is humility that, although the Devil seems to mimic all virtues, he does not begin to understand the nature of this one. The Apostle, however, with his knowledge of the protection it offers and the stability, instructs us to clothe ourselves in it and to wrap it about ourselves (cf. Pet 5: 5), even while we are performing all our worthwhile acts.[58] If you are fasting, for example, or giving alms, or teaching, and if, moreover, you are self-controlled and understanding, still you should establish this virtue in yourself as an unassailable defensive wall. Let this fairest of all virtues, humility, bind you together and contain your virtues. You know also the hymn of the three holy children (Dan 3: 87); without mentioning any of the other virtues at all, they number the humble with those who sing hymns, without mentioning the prudent or the poor. For just as it is impossible for a ship to be built without nails, so it is impossible to be saved without humility.

57

"Because humility is good and salutary, the Lord clothed himself in it while fulfilling the economy [of salvation] for humanity. For he says: *Learn from me, for I am gentle and humble of heart* (Mt 11: 29).[59] Notice who it is who is speaking; learn his lesson perfectly. Let humility become for you the beginning and end of virtues. He means a humble heart; he refers not to appearance alone, but to the inner person, for the outer person will also follow after the inner. Have you observed all the commandments? The Lord knows, but he personally commands you to take up again the rule of servitude. For he says: *When you have done all these things, say: 'We are useless servants'* (Lk 17: 10).

58

"Humility, then, is formed through rebukes, through insults, through blows; you hear yourself called mindless and stupid, poor and a beggar, weak and worthless, ineffectual in what you do and irrational in what you say, contemptible in appearance, weak in power. These insults are the sinews of humility. These our Lord heard and experienced, for they said he was *a Samaritan* and was *possessed* (cf. Jn 8: 48). He took on *the form of a slave* (cf. Phil 2: 6), he was beaten, he was humiliated with blows (cf. Mt 26: 67; Isa 50: 6).

59

"And so we must imitate this humility that he put into practice. There are some, you see, who feign humility through their outward appearance and submissive manner, but who are seeking fame by this very behaviour. But they are known from their fruits (cf. Mt 7: 16); for in fact, when mildly insulted, they do not tolerate it, but immediately, like serpents, they spew forth their venom."[60]

60

And the women who had gathered there rejoiced greatly at these words and yet still remained since they had not received their fill of her good advice. And again the blessed woman spoke to them. "For those who are making their way to God there is at first great struggle and effort, but then indescribable joy. For just as those who wish to kindle a fire are at first choked with smoke, suffer watery eyes, and in this way achieve their purpose (indeed Scripture says: *Our God is a consuming fire* [Heb 12: 29]), so we too must kindle the divine fire within us with tears and effort.[61] The Lord himself says: *I came to cast fire on the earth* (Lk 12: 49). Some, too, through their remissness, have endured the smoke, but have not kindled the fire because they did not have the perseverance and, even more, because their attachment to the Divine was tenuous and uncertain.

61

"Love, then, is a great treasure; and about this virtue the Apostle spoke strongly: *If you distribute all your goods, and if you discipline your body, but have not love, you are sounding brass and clanging cymbal* (cf. 1 Cor 13: 1–3). And so, among the virtues love is paramount, as among the vices anger is likewise pre-eminent.[62] For, after rendering the soul totally dark and inhuman, anger destroys reason. But the Lord, ever solicitous for our salvation, has not allowed so much as a speck of our soul to remain unprotected. Does the Enemy provoke lust? The Lord has armed us with self-control.[63] Does he engender pride? Well, humility is not far distant. Has he infused hatred? Well, love is in our midst. Whatever weapons, therefore, the Enemy hurls at us, the Lord has protected us with stronger armour both for our salvation and for the downfall of that Foe.

62

"Vice among vices, however, is anger;[64] for, Scripture says, *a man's wrath does not produce God's justice* (cf. Jas 1: 20). We must, then, 'rein it in', because on occasion it has been seen to be useful; for to feel anger and be provoked against demons is proper. But it is not appropriate to be strongly aroused against a human, even if he happens to have committed an offense; on the contrary, one ought to reform the person after the passion of anger has ceased.

63

"However, to be angry is, as it were, a minor vice, whereas remembrance of wrongs is the most serious of all. For anger, like smoke, disappears once it has disturbed the soul for a while, but remembrance of wrongs, as if embedded in the soul, renders it more formidable than a wild beast. Even a dog, enraged against someone, relinquishes its anger when coaxed with a tidbit; and the other beasts also become gentle with habit. One who is governed by remembrance of wrongs, however, is not persuaded by entreaty, nor made gentle by food, nor indeed does time that transforms all things heal the suffering of such a person. These people, then, are the most impious of all and the most lawless, for they do not obey the Saviour when he says: *First go and be reconciled to your brother and in this condition make your offering* (cf. Mt 5: 24). And elsewhere Scripture says: *Do not let the sun set on your anger* (cf. Eph 4: 26).

64

"It is good, therefore, not to be angry; but, if it does happen, the Apostle allows you not so much as the span of a day for your emotion, for he says that *the sun is not to set [on your anger]*. You, however, keep delaying until your life span has 'set.' You do not know how to say: *Sufficient for the day is its own evil* (cf. Mt 6:34). Why do you hate the person who has vexed you? He was not the one who wronged you, but the Devil. Hate the disease and not the one who is sick.[65] Why do you exalt in evil, O powerful one (cf. Ps 52: 1; LXX 51: 3)? The psalm has proclaimed this about you when it says: For you plotted lawlessness the whole day (cf. Ps 52: 3–4; LXX 51: 2–3). That is, for the whole span of your life you disobey the Lawmaker when he says: Let not the sun set on your anger. And Scripture says: Your tongue has plotted unrighteousness (cf. Ps 52: 2; LXX 51: 4), for you do not cease speaking evil of your brother. Therefore, in your case, the vengeance pronounced by the Psalmist himself under the influence of the Spirit is justified; he says: Therefore God will destroy you in the end; may he snatch you out and remove you from your tent and your root from the land of the living (cf. Ps 52: 5; LXX 51: 7). These punishments are the rewards for the one who remembers wrongs, these the prizes for this vice.

65

"It is essential, then, to be on guard against remembrance of wrongs, for many terrible consequences develop from it: envy, sadness, malicious talk. The evil of these vices is lethal, even if they seem to occur in small doses. For these are, so to speak, the light weaponry of the Enemy. Moreover, often the wounds from the two-edged blade and the larger sword (such as sexual impurity, greed, and murder) have been healed through the saving medicine of conversion. Pride, however, or remembrance of wrongs or malicious talk (which seem to be, figuratively speaking, small weapons) have wrought destruction unnoticed, once they have been implanted in the more vital parts of the soul. And these vices do damage not by the size of their blow, but by the negligence of the wounded. For, since they consider malicious talk and the rest as of no significance, they perish from them little by little.

66

"Malicious talk, therefore, is a serious and troublesome matter, for it is the sustenance and recreation of some people. You should not, however, accept empty hearsay, lest you become a receptacle for other peoples' evils. Keep your own soul unlittered. For, [my sister],[66] by accepting the foul-smelling garbage of words, you will introduce stains to your prayer through your thoughts, and without cause you will hate your associates. For when your hearing has been drenched with the misanthropy of malicious talkers, you will look on all people without generosity; just as the eye has a blurred image of objects seen when it is inordinately obsessed with colour.

67

"We must, then, guard our tongue and hearing against saying or listening to any such matter willingly. *For it has been written: Do not receive empty hearsay* (cf. Ex 23: 1) and *The one who secretly slanders his neighbour–him I banished* (cf. Ps 101: 5; LXX 100: 5). In the Psalmist also it says: *May my mouth not talk about the works of mortals* (cf. Ps 17: 4; LXX 16: 4).[67] But we also talk about the "non-works." We must not believe, therefore the things that are said, nor indeed judge the speakers, but we must act and speak according to Holy Scripture. *But I, like a deaf person, did not hear, and, like a mute, I did not open my mouth* (cf. Ps 17: 4; LXX 16: 4).[68]

68

"We should not take joy in the misfortune of a human being, even if he is very sinful. When some people see a person being whipped or, imprisoned, they quote in their ignorance that folk maxim that says: The one who has arranged [his cushions] badly will be uncomfortable at the banquet.[69] You, then, [my sister],[70] who have arranged your affairs well, are you confident that you have found peace in life? And what shall we do about the one who says: *There is one outcome for the just and for the sinner* (cf. Eccl 9: 2)? For our human condition is the same, even if we practise a different way of life.

69

"We must not hate our enemies. The Lord, in fact, gave us this commandment in his own words, for he says: *Do not love only those who love you; for this even sinners and tax collectors do* (cf. Mt 5: 46). The pursuit of good does not require craft or contest, for it attracts to itself those who love it. The abandonment of evil, on the other hand, does require inspired teaching and much effort. For the kingdom of heaven belongs not to the relaxed and negligent, but to the forceful (cf Mt 11: 12).

70

"And so, just as we must not hate our enemies, so we must not shun or mock the negligent and indolent. Some people, therefore, set before themselves that Scriptural passage that says: *You will be holy with the holy and you will bend with the crooked* (cf. Ps 18: 25–26; LXX 17: 26–27).[71] In this passage, Scripture says, we flee sinners to avoid being bent by them. In the ignorance of their souls, such people do the opposite. For Holy Scripture bids us not to be bent with the crooked, but to straighten them from their crookedness. *You will bend* means *you will draw him* to yourself, from the left to the right.

71

"Regarding the life of humans there are three categories of dispositions: the first of these is characterised by extreme wickedness; the second is characterised by a kind of middle viewpoint, for it looks, so to speak, at both attitudes while sharing in each; but the third category, led into profound contemplation, manages not only itself, but attempts to guide gently the two categories behind. Evil people, therefore, by mingling with those even worse, create a large increase in terrible people. Those of the middle category try to avoid undisciplined people through fear of this very thing—that they might be dragged down again by them – for they are still like children in matters of virtue. Those of the third category, however, courageous in disposition and strong in will, live with the weak and share their lives in their desire to save them.[72] And, to be sure, they are censured by people on the outside and mocked by those who see them spending their lives with people less disciplined; in fact, people slander them as if they were similar. Nevertheless, the people of this third category carry out their divinely appointed work freely, interpreting the rebukes of others as praises; for Scripture says: *Rejoice and be glad when people say every manner of lie against you* (cf. Mt 5: 11–12). The behaviour of the people of this category is like the Lord's, for the

Lord ate with tax collectors and sinners (cf. Mt 9: 11). Their attitude is characterised by brotherly love rather than self-love, for they regard those who sin as houses on fire; giving no thought to their own interests, they apply their efforts to save what belongs to others and is being destroyed, and, though scorched by fiery insults, they persist. But the people of the middle category flee if they see their brother being singed by sin, in fear lest the fire spread also to them. And as for the people of the first category,[73] they act like bad neighbours and light more fires under those already in flames, supplying for their destruction their own evil as the actual firewood. As if coming upon a boat smeared with pitch, they throw cedar oil upon it instead of water. But in complete contrast to these, good people have placed their own possessions second to the salvation of others. This is the sign of genuine love; these people are the custodians of pure love.

72

"Just as dreadful qualities are attached to one another (for example, envy follows upon avarice, as do treachery, perjury, anger, and remembrance of wrongs), so the opposite qualities of these vices are dependent upon love; I mean, of course, gentleness and patience, as well as endurance, and the ultimate good – holy poverty. It is not possible for anyone to acquire this virtue (I mean, to be sure, love) apart from holy poverty, for the Lord did not enjoin love on one person, but on all.[74] Those, therefore, who have resources must not overlook those who have needs. The workings of love, in fact, are concealed, for it is impossible for a human being to supply the needs for all, but this is the task of God.

73

"Why, then, (she says) do you who possess nothing agonise over almsgiving? And why does this matter of almsgiving become a pretext for acquisition? This commandment to give alms has been issued to secular people, for almsgiving has been instituted not so much for the nourishing of the poor person as for the sake of love. God who manages affairs for the rich person also nourishes the poor. Well, then, was almsgiving enjoined for no purpose? Of course not! On the contrary, it is the beginning of love for those who do not know love. Just as circumcision was symbolic of circumcision of the heart, so also has almsgiving been established as a teacher of love. For those, therefore, to whom love has been given by grace, almsgiving is superfluous.

74

"I am saying this not to belittle mercy, but to show the purity of holy poverty. May the smaller virtue not become a hindrance to the greater one! You have quickly straightened out the small virtue for you have given away everything all at once. From this day forward look to the greater virtue – love; for you have taken up the cross. You ought to quote the proclamation of freedom: *Lo, we have left all and followed you* (cf. Mt 19: 27). You have been deemed worthy to echo the confident statement of the Apostles, for Peter and John say: *Gold and silver I do not have* (cf. Acts 3: 6). That statement came from two people, but their faith was of one kind.

75

"Even among secular people almsgiving should not be practised indiscriminately in this respect. For Scripture says: *Let not the oil of a sinner anoint my head* (Ps 141: 5; LXX 140: 5). It is fitting, therefore, for the almsgiver to have the attitude of Abraham and, like him, to do justice justly; for the just man, while offering hospitality, exposed his outlook along with the food. For Scripture says: *He stood serving, not wanting his servants to share in his reward* (cf. Gen 18: 8). Truly, such people will have their reward for almsgiving, even if they are in the second rank. In creating the world, the Lord established in it two ranks of inhabitants. For some who live pious lives he decreed marriage for the sake of making children; but for others he decreed holiness through chastity of life, making them like angels. And to the former he gave laws, punishments, and instructions, but to the latter he says: *Punishment belongs to me; I will give retribution, says the Lord* (Rom 12: 19; cf. Deut 32: 35). To the first group he says: *You will work the earth* (cf. Gen 3: 23). The second group he bids: *Take no thought for the morrow* (cf. Mt 6: 34). To the first group he gave law; but to us he revealed his commandment openly through grace.

76

"The cross is for us the trophy of victory. For our calling is nothing other than a renunciation of life, a rehearsal of death.[75] Just as corpses, then, are not active in their body, so we too. Whatever there was to accomplish through the body, we have done when we were children. For the Apostle says: *The world has been crucified to me, and I to the world* (cf. Gal 6: 14). We live by the soul; by it let us demonstrate our virtues. Let us show mercy in our heart, *for blessed are the merciful* (Mt 5: 27) in soul. As Scripture says in the following: *The man who has lusted after a beautiful body, even without the act, has committed sin unwitnessed* (Mt 5: 27). So here almsgiving is meant: when the will performs the deed, even if the money is lacking, we are rewarded with greater value.

77

"For secular lords procure various services from their domestics. Some they send out in their country holdings to work the land and to safeguard the succession of their kind; but, if they see any of their servants' progeny that are suitable and comely, they transfer them to their own houses for their personal service. So also the Lord has placed on his 'country estate' of the world those who have chosen for themselves honourable marriage; but the more distinguished progeny of these people – especially those who have the proper predisposition – he has stationed close to himself for service. These are unfamiliar with earthly concerns, for they have been deemed worthy of the Master's table. They do not care about clothing (cf. Mt 6: 25), for they have 'put on' (cf. Gal 3: 27) Christ.

78

"Of both ranks, then, there is one master – the Lord. For just as within the same grain plant there is both the chaff and the seed, so from the same God there are both people who live devoutly in the world and people who have chosen the solitary life. And, to be sure, there is a need for both, since foliage is needed for the support and protection of the seed, and the production of fruit is also necessary, for the fruit is the source of the whole process. Just as it is not possible to be both herbage and seed at the same time, so it is impossible to make heavenly fruit with the splendour of the world all around us.[76] But when the greenery falls away and the stalk has dried up, the head of the grain is ready for harvest. And so, [sisters][77] in our case: after we have cast off the illusion of the world (the foliage, so to speak) and have withered in the body (like the plant stalk), and once we have raised up our thoughts, we shall be able to produce the 'seed' of salvation.

79

"It is dangerous for someone not 'formed' by experience of the ascetic life to try to teach; it is as if someone whose house is unsound were to receive guests and cause them injury by the collapse of the building. In the same way these people also destroy along with themselves those who have come to them, by not first building securely their own way of life. With their words they called to salvation their followers, but with the evilness of their way of life they instead did them harm.[78] For the mere articulation of words is like inscriptions painted in perishable colours which a very short period of time has destroyed with blasts of wind and splashes of rain. Teaching that is based on ascetic experience, on the other hand, not even all eternity could destroy. By chiselling away the rough edges of the soul, the spoken word bestows on the faithful Christ's everlasting image done in stone.

80

"We ought not, therefore, make our treatment of the soul superficial, but we ought to put our soul in order throughout, paying particular attention to its depths. We have our hair cut off; at the same time let us remove also the 'lice' on our head, for by themselves these will cause us still more grief, Our 'hair,' you see, was the worldly element in life: honours, fame, possession of goods, splendid outfits of clothing, use of baths, enjoyment of foods. These we thought it wise to discard; but rather let us cast off the soul-devouring 'lice,' some of which are these: slander, perjury, avarice.[79] Our 'head,' then, is the soul; as long as the 'beasties'[80] were sheltered in the 'forest' of worldly affairs, they seemed to escape notice, but now, stripped of cover, they are visible to all. For this reason, in a nun or a monk, even the minor sins are conspicuous; just as in a clean house a 'beastie,' even if it is very small, is obvious to all once it has been spotted. Among secular people, however, the largest of venomous 'beasties' go unnoticed, lurking, so to speak, in filthy lairs where they are concealed by the dense 'forest.' We must, then, keep cleaning our 'house' continually and be on the lookout lest any of the soul-devouring 'beasties' slip past us into the storerooms of the soul. And we must fumigate our places with the holy incense of prayer. For just as the stronger fumigants drive out the venomous creatures, so prayer with fasting chases out foul patterns of thought.

81

"One of the soul-devouring 'beasties' is also the undermining that is caused by those who say that Destiny exists, which they call *genesis*.[81] This too is a goad of the Devil – a very terrible one. For zealous souls, on the one hand, it often flits away, after stirring up in the mind no more than a pestilential illusion; but, on the other hand, it takes control of more negligent souls. Of those who live according to virtue no one believes or accepts this mind-damaging and false concept; for such people believe that God is the source of all good present and past, and they place second the individual will as the instigator and judge of virtue and vice. But all those who have suffered from lack of will and from laziness immediately encounter that demonic concept. Like children who run away and refuse to endure the training given them by their parents for their good, they come to desert places in their wanderings and encounter wild and savage demons. Because they are ashamed to make their own attitude the cause of their actions, they falsely accuse a force that does not exist.

82

"After pushing themselves still further from the Divine, to be sure, they say that the life of pleasure was imposed on them by their destiny-at-birth;[82] for in the midst of sexual activity and theft, ill with avarice and deceitfulness, shamed at their own deeds, they turn away from truth. The end of their point of view is a despair that is fatal for them; as a result of these thoughts God is necessarily eliminated from their lives and even more his judgement. They say: 'If this decision has been made for me – to be a fornicator or a miser – then judgement is superfluous. For a vengeance that is just is appropriate for voluntary sins; but the involuntary act arising out of some unknown origin renders the doer blameless, and for this reason the judgement is inappropriate.'

83

"And how the Divine also is rejected by them must be heard. For they will say in their foolishness that the Divine is first, or second, or ever co-existent. If, then, they say that God is first, it will necessarily follow that everything has its origin in him; and, in fact, he is present in all. He is, therefore, himself the Lord of Destiny. If, moreover, one is greedy or lustful as a result of his destiny-at-birth, God is necessarily the cause of evil through the medium of destiny-at-birth – an absurd conclusion! But if they assert again that the Divine is second, reason requires that it is subservient to the first. And whatever the leading element wills, the subsequent element will perforce follow. And so again, in their view, God is the cause of evil – an inadmissible conclusion! If, however, they mean that the Divine is co-eternal, they will raise an all-out battle between two principles with opposing natures. From these arguments, then, their groundless conjecture is summarily overturned. Scripture has spoken about these matters when it says: *The foolish man said in his heart, there is no God* (Ps 14: 1; LXX 13: 1); and *They have spoken wickedness to the heights* (cf. Ps 73: 8 (LXX 72: 8).

84

"They are, of course, making excuses for themselves in their sins. In their blindness, indeed, they mutilate Scripture through their desire to confirm their wrongheadedness by means of it. First, moreover, it is from the Gospel that they force their meaning as they attempt to spew forth their poison; for the Gospel says: *The genesis of Christ was as follows* (Mt 1: 18).[83] In fact, Holy Scripture did term his birth genesis. Still, his coming into being among humans according to Providence has been named genesis (destiny-at-birth) with good reason. But if, however, they speak falsely also about the star,[84] in that passage also let them learn again of his glorious coming. For us one exceedingly bright star became a herald of truth, but their foolish opinion leads many into a hunt for a human genesis (destiny-at-birth).

And as a result it has been demonstrated that evil everywhere contradicts itself. They also call Isaiah to witness to their foolishness, for they say that he has said: The Lord is the one who makes peace and creates evil (Isa 45: 7). Hence peace is proclaimed among all as a work of God; but evil, on the other hand, actually resides among them, occurring as evil of the soul. Among us, however, the evil originating from God is very beneficial; for famines and droughts, plagues and poverty, and other misfortunes are for the salvation of the soul and the training of the body. These saving remedies (which those people falsely regard as evil of the soul and as evils) are offered to us for our conversion by the Almighty. *For what son is there that a father does not discipline* (cf. Heb 12: 7)? And again this passage: Man's paths are not in his control (cf. Jer 10: 23). Once more, in the same way, these misinterpretations lead to personal disaster, for, although they do not have 'paths', they wish to find them. Greed, or gluttony, or sexual impurity do not offer a 'path', for these vices are without substance since they do not exist in themselves. Yet those people customarily call these vices a 'path'. Scripture, however, tells us that there are two 'paths' common to all: life and death. For they are in truth the avenues of entrance into this world and of passing over from these visible realms.

85

"The unfortunate wretches, then, do everything to remove themselves from free will[85] and they apply this zealousness to exchanging their freedom for slavery. (This, indeed, is the function of evil: to drag itself down to an even lower level.) They become their own witnesses to having sold themselves to evil. Even this is the deceptive device of the Devil, for he makes negligent souls ready to journey downwards through false doctrine, while refusing to allow them to climb back up to an acknowledgement of truth. Just as a ship sailing without rudders is constantly tossed about, so is danger ever gusting against them; nor are they able to reach a safe harbour since they have dropped the Lord as their pilot. Thus the Devil leads astray the souls committed to him. Often also, the Enemy ambushes the zealous through these very techniques, in his desire to cut off their virtuous course. He suggests to their thoughts that success arises from the movement of the stars. This notion the Adversary introduced to those who have turned away from worldly wisdom to the solitary life; for the Devil, cunning in his wiles, lays his snares to fit the natures of people. For some he is ever present in their despair; some he drags down in their vainglory, and others he 'buries' through their avarice. Like a death-dealing doctor, he brings poison to people: one person he destroys through the liver,[86] by offering to him the venom of lust; while another he makes sick at heart by directing his passion toward anger; and for some he blunts their guiding faculty,[87] either by enveloping them in ignorance or by distracting them with idle curiosity.

86

"He has diverted some by means of their devious inquiries; for in their desire to understand about God and his essence, they foundered. Without having sufficiently mastered the practical side of ascetic life, they rushed into contemplation and, overcome by dizziness, have fallen. Since they did not take up the first in its proper order, they failed at the second. Similarly, those who happen upon the letter alpha, first see its shape, and second they are taught its name, and in the same way they learn its numerical significance, and finally they acquire the pitches. If, then, over the first letter there is such a great need for practice and skill, how much more, in the case of the Creator, should effort and time precede the contemplation of him who has merited indescribable glory? Yet one should not pride oneself on a comprehension of the Divine when one is making one's start from pagan learning. Such a person deceived himself, since he is deluded by the Devil. For the Psalmist says: *Out of the mouths of babes and sucklings have you fashioned your praise* (cf. Ps 8: 2; LXX 8: 3). And the Lord says in the Gospel: *Suffer little children to come to me, for of such is the kingdom of heaven* (cf. Lk 18: 16). Elsewhere also he says: Unless you become as little children, you will not enter into the kingdom of heaven (cf. Mt 18: 3). You were taught these lessons for the sake of the world; become a fool for the sake of God (cf. 1 Cor 3: 8). Cut back the old growth, that you may plant new growth. Destroy the unsound foundations, that you may replace them with the indestructible underpinning of the Lord, so that you too, like the Apostles, may be built on solid rock (cf. Mt 16: 18).

87

"There is no need, then, to be quarrelsome; do not spend long periods of time in extended conversations, for the Devil can actually do harm through inopportune chit chat. He has many snares and is a formidable hunter; for the tiniest of sparrows, for example, he makes small traps, but for large birds he prepares strong snares. An important and lethal snare is the belief that *genesis* [destiny-at-birth] exists. Thinking along these lines is to be avoided. Does the Devil, however, persuade you through actual events and foreknowledge? The method is based on conjecture, the rationale is unreliable. For what is said by seers does not necessarily happen. Just as some uneducated people and sailors have a kind of a hazy knowledge of winds or rainstorms from the character of the clouds, so also these people have a confused foreknowledge from demons. Actually they make some prophecies by guesswork, as also do mediums.[88] This consideration could greatly weaken their feeble argument; for if their conjectures themselves are lies from demons, then the 'craft' of those who make predictions is useless.

88

But if the Enemy continues pleading his cause still more in these matters, you will refute him on this ground: that at one time he battles with the soul with one argument and at another time with another argument. What is inconstant is unsound, and what is unsound is close to perdition. Nor is the Devil satisfied with his first evil, but indeed he also suggests to the soul an automatic functioning of nature,[89] and he labels the mind that is our guide as a 'blossom' of nature; he says, furthermore, that when the body disintegrates, the soul also perishes with it. All these ideas he suggests to us with a view to destroying the soul through negligence. But when these dismal illusions are present, let us not assent to them as to truths. For these illusions manifest their evil, approaching at one time in one way and at another time in another way – *flitting by in the twinkling of an eye* (1 Cor 15: 52). In fact, I know a servant of God living according to virtue who, while sitting in his cell, observed the occurrences of evil thoughts and kept track of which came first and which second, and of how long a time each one of them persisted, and of whether it occurred later or earlier than on the preceding day. Thus he came to know accurately the grace of God and his own strength and power, and eventually, to be sure, he came to know also the overthrow of the Enemy.

89

We must, therefore, keep these rules which have been received. If those who traffic in perishable merchandise count their profits and joyfully welcome their gains and are distressed at their losses, it is much more fitting for those who traffic in genuine treasure to be alert and to strive for more virtues. And if there should be even some small theft by the Enemy, it is proper to take it seriously because of the judgement, but not, certainly, to become despondent and toss away everything because of an involuntary lapse. You have ninety-nine sheep – seek also the one that is lost (cf. Lk 15: 4)! But do not panic because of that one, lest you run away from the Master, and the bloodsucking Devil will take captive and destroy the whole 'flock' of your good deeds. Do not, then, desert because of the one sheep, for the Master is good; he says through the Psalmist: *If he falls, he will not be broken, because the Lord holds him by the hand* (cf. Ps 37: 24; LXX 36: 24).

90

"Whatever we do or gain in this world, let us consider it insignificant in comparison to the eternal wealth that is to come. We are on this earth as if in a second maternal womb. In that inner recess we did not have a life such as we have here, for we did not have there solid nourishment such as we enjoy now, nor were we able to be active, indeed, as we are here, and we in fact existed without the light of the sun and of any glimmer of light. Just as, then, when we were in that inner chamber, we did without many of the things of this world, so also in the present world we are impoverished in comparison with the kingdom of heaven. We have sampled the nourishment here; let us reach for the Divine! We have enjoyed the light in this world; let us long for *the sun of righteousness* (cf. Mal 4: 2)! Let us regard *the heavenly Jerusalem* (Gal 4: 26) as our homeland and our mother, and let us call God our father. Let us live prudently in this world that we may obtain eternal life.

91

"Once babes in their mother's womb have been brought to full development on the basis of a considerably reduced nourishment and vitality, they are brought through this state and into an improved condition of health. So also the just withdraw from the life of the world to the journey of ascent according to Scripture: *From strength to strength [they will go]* (Ps 84: 7; LXX 83: 8). Sinners, on the other hand, are given over from darkness to darkness, like embryos that have died in the mother's womb. They are actually dead on earth, smothered by the multitude of their sins, and once they have been taken from this life, they are led down to the realms of darkness and hell. Three times we are born to life. The first of these births is the passage from our mothers' wombs, when we are brought from earth to earth; the remaining two lead us from earth up to heaven. The first one of this second group is by grace which comes to us from holy baptism and this birth we rightly call 'being born again.' The third birth is granted to us as a result of our conversion and good works. We are at present in this third stage.

92

"When we have drawn near to the true bridegroom, [sisters],[90] we ought to be suitably outfitted. The spectacle of a secular marriage should be a model for us. If those women who are matched to an easily-acquired mortal put so much enthusiasm into baths, ointments, and various adornments (for with these they fancy that they render themselves more lovable), and if so powerful a vision is engendered for those who live according to the flesh, how much more should we surpass those women in will. We who are betrothed to the Heavenly Bridegroom ought also to wash away the filth of our sins with strenuous discipline and to exchange our bodily garments for spiritual ones. Those women deck the body with worldly adornments and with flowers from the earth; let us brighten up our souls with virtues. And instead of precious stones, let us encircle our head with the triple crown of faith, hope, and charity; and about our throat let us place the precious necklace of humility. Instead of a belt, let us gird ourselves with chastity, and let our glistening robe be poverty. And let there be brought forth for the wedding feast imperishable delicacies–prayers and psalms. But as the Apostle says: Do not move only your tongue, but also consider with the spirit what is being said. For often the mouth speaks, but the heart is busy with distracting thoughts (cf. 1 Cor 14: 14–15). It is necessary, moreover, to pay attention lest we who have drawn near the divine nuptials suffer from too few 'lamps,' that is too few virtues. For our Betrothed will give us neither love nor welcome if he does not receive what we have promised. And what are these promises? To think less of the body and to tend[91] the soul more – this is the one covenant we have with him.

93

"Just as it is not possible to bring up at the same time two buckets filled with water since, by the turning of the windlass, the one bucket is lowered empty and the other is brought up full, so it is in our case. When we apply to the soul total concern, it is brought up filled with virtues and pointed towards heaven. And our body (which has become light through discipline) does not weigh down the leading force [of the counterbalance]. And of this the Apostle is witness for he says: *Inasmuch as our outer person is destroyed, so much is the inner person renewed* (cf. 2 Cor 4: 16).

94

"Do you live in a cenobitic monastery? Do not change your location, for you will be greatly harmed. For just as a bird that abandons its eggs renders them empty and unfruitful, so a nun or a monk grows cold and dies to faith by moving from place to place.[92]

95

"Let not the delights of those who are wealthy by worldly standards entice you as being something useful. For the sake of pleasure they honour the culinary art; by fasting and through frugality surpass their superabundance of foodstuffs. For Scripture says: *A soul, when satisfied, scorns honey* (Prov 27: 7). Do not fill up with bread and you will not crave wine.[93]

96

"The main sources of the Enemy from which every evil springs are threefold: desire, pleasure, sadness. These are connected one from another, and one follows another. It is possible to control pleasure to some extent, but impossible to control desire; for the end of pleasure is achieved through the body, but that [of desire][94] originates from the soul, while sadness is concocted from both. Well then, do not allow desire to become active, and you will dissipate the remaining two. But if you permit the first to emerge, it will develop into the second and they will form with one another 'a vicious circle;'[95] and in no way will the soul be allowed to escape. For Scripture says: *Do not grant a way out to water* (Sir 25: 25).

97

"Not all courses are suitable for all people. Each person should have confidence in his own disposition, because for many it is profitable to live in a community And over others it is helpful to withdraw on their own. For just as some plants become more flourishing when they are in humid locations, while others are more stable in drier conditions, so also among humans, some flourish in the higher places, while others achieve salvation in the lower places. Many people, then, have found salvation in a city, while imagining the conditions of a desert. And many, though on a mountain, have been lost by living the life of townspeople. It is possible for one who is in a group to be alone in thought, and for one who is alone to live mentally with a crowd.[96]

98

"Many are the goads of the Devil. Has he not altered a soul through poverty? He introduces wealth as an enticement. Has he not shown strength through insults and rebukes? He offers praises and glory. Has he been bested by good health? He makes the body sick. When he has been unable to lead a person astray by pleasures, he tries to bring about the soul's perversion, unchosen and unwanted, by involuntary hardships. He introduces as needed[97] some diseases (and very serious ones too) so that those weakened by these diseases may falter in their love of God. But if your body is being slashed and is on fire with raging fevers and is being weighed down with an unquenchable and intolerable thirst, if you, sinner that you are, have endured these tortures, remember the punishment to come, both the eternal fire and the penalties demanded by justice – and you will not weaken in the face of the present circumstances. Rejoice because the Lord has watched over you, and keep on your tongue that holy saying: *The Lord has chastened me sorely, but has not given me over to the death of sin* (cf. Ps 118: 18; LXX 117: 8). You were [already] iron; well, through fire you lose your rust! And even if you fall ill, though you are a just person, you progress from great virtue to greater! You are [already] gold; well, through fire you become more valuable! There has been given to you in your flesh a messenger of Satan (cf. 2 Cor 12: 7; consider whom you resemble! For you have been deemed worthy of the gift of Paul. You are being tested by burning heat; you are being disciplined through cold; but Scripture says: *We passed through fire and water* (Ps 66: 12; LXX 65: 12). Hereafter a resting place has been prepared. You have experienced the first; expect the second. While practising your virtue,[98] cry out the words of holy David, for he says: *I am a pauper, and a beggar, and I am afflicted* (cf. Ps 69: 29; LXX 68: 30).[99] You will become perfect through these three. In fact, Scripture says: *In affliction you made me grow* (cf. Ps 4: 1; LXX 4: 2).[100] By these exercises especially let us train our souls, for we see the Adversary before our very eyes.[101]

99

"Let us not be saddened if we are unable to stand for prayer or to sing Psalms aloud because of the frailty and affliction of our body; all these ailments have been brought to pass for us for the destruction of our desires. Actually, fasting and sleeping on the ground have been prescribed for us because of shameful pleasures. If, then, disease has dulled these pleasures, austerity is superfluous. But why do I say superfluous? Because potentially fatal lapses have been checked by illness as if by some strong and powerful medication. This is the great ascesis: to remain strong in illness and to keep sending up hymns of thanksgiving to the Almighty.[102] Are we deprived of our eyes? Let us not take it amiss; we have lost the instruments of insatiable desire, and yet with our inner eyes we contemplate as in a mirror the glory of the Lord (cf. 2 Cor 3: 18). Have we been struck deaf? Let us give thanks that we have completely lost useless noise. Have we suffered damage to our hands? Nonetheless we still have our inner hands well prepared for war against the Enemy. Is illness in control throughout our whole body? Still, the health of the inner person (cf. Rom 7: 22) will increase all the more.

100

"When we live in community, [sisters],[103] let us choose obedience over discipline; for the latter teaches arrogance, while the former calls for humility.[104] There is also a discipline that is encouraged by the Enemy. His disciples, in fact, practise this discipline. How, then, are we to discern the divine and royal discipline from the tyrannical and demonical? It is obvious: we discern them by moderation. For you, through your whole life, there should be a single rule for fasting. Do not fast for four or five days and on the next day dissipate your strength with a surplus of foods. This backsliding is sweet for the Enemy. At all times a lack of moderation is destructive. Do not expend all your defensive weapons at one time; you will be caught unarmed and will become a prisoner in the war. Our armour is the body and our soul is the soldier; take care of them both against the time of need. When you are young and healthy, fast; for old age will come with its frailty. To the best of your ability store resources, so that you may find them when you are weak.[105] Fast reasonably and yet scrupulously. Watch that the Enemy not become involved in the business of your fasting. I think that perhaps the Saviour was speaking about this in the following: Be good money changers (cf. Mt 25: 27).[106] That is, learn to know the royal stamp exactly; for there are counterfeit stamps. The nature of the gold is the same, but there is a difference in the impression.[107] The 'gold' is fasting, self-control, and almsgiving; but the followers of the Greeks have stamped on these virtues the image of their tyrant, and all heretics honour this false currency because of the Greeks. But you must be on the alert for these false coins and flee them as counterfeit. You have to be careful lest you pay a penalty for coming upon them without training. Receive, therefore, in safety the cross of Christ imprinted with virtues; that is, correct faith with holy deeds.

101

"It is essential for us to govern our soul with all discretion, and, since we live in community, [sisters],[108] not to seek our own interest, or to be slaves to our own will, but to obey our spiritual-mother in faith.[109] We have committed ourselves to exile, that is, we are outside secular boundaries; we have, then, been banished – let us not seek the same ends. In the world we had good repute; here we have rebuke. There we had an abundance of food; here a deficiency even of bread. In the world, those who stumble, even involuntarily, are thrown into prison. Let us likewise imprison ourselves for our sins so that the voluntary gesture of our will may stave off future punishment.

102

"Are you fasting? Do not use illness as a pretext [to stop]. Actually, those who are not fasting fall victim to the same diseases. Have you made a start in the virtuous life? Do not bolt when the Enemy checks you; for he himself is confounded by your steadfastness. Those who are beginning a sea voyage first encounter a favouring wind when they have unfurled their sails, but later a contrary wind blows against them; the sailors, however, do not dock the ship on account of a fortuitous breeze, but they continue their voyage after lying quiet for a little while or even after having battled against the storm blast. So we too shall complete our voyage successfully when we encounter an opposing wind, if we raise the cross in place of the sail."[110]

103

These are the teachings of the holy and saintly Syncletica, but they are more her practices than her words. Other teachings also, numerous and important, were promulgated by her as a help for those who listened to her and observed her. So great a profusion of good teachings flowed forth from her that the human tongue would be at a loss to tell them all.

104

The Devil, who hates good, was shrivelling up since he was unable to tolerate so great an abundance of goodness, and he kept trying to devise a scenario in his mind whereby he could thwart the progress of her virtues. Finally he challenged that most noble virgin to the ultimate contest. Because of his hatred, moreover, he wreaked such savage vengeance on her that he did not commence his assault on her external members, but apportioned to her pain deep within by assailing her innards so that she could not be comforted by human help.

105

First he strikes the part most essential for life – the lung – and through fatal diseases applies his evil little by little. He was allowed, actually, to cut short her end at his choice, but, like a bloodthirsty executioner, he demonstrated his cruelty through many afflictions and over a long time. By breaking her lung up bit by bit with the phlegm she coughed up, he gradually removed it. In addition, unremitting fevers persisted, wearing her body away like a file.

106

She was in her eightieth year when the Devil transferred to her the trials of Job, for on that occasion also he used the same scourges, although in the present case he cut down[III] the time by making the pains more severe. Blessed Job completed thirty-five years in his affliction, but in this situation the Enemy took away three decades as an offering of first-fruits, so to speak, and applied them to the afflictions of this woman's holy body. For three and a half years she battled against the Enemy by means of these renowned sufferings. And so, in the case of Job, the Devil initiated wounds from the outside, but in the case of this woman, he assailed her with torments from wounds on the inside; for by afflicting her inner organs, he allotted to her more severe and arduous suffering. I do not think that the noblest martyrs suffered as bravely as did the celebrated Syncletica, for the Avenger attacked them externally. Even if he brought the sword against them, even if he brought fire, it was gentler than the trials she experienced. He burned her innards as if in a fiery furnace, lighting the fire from within little by little, and like a file he wore away her body over a long period of time. It is truly grievous and inhumane to speak of this process. Whenever those who have been entrusted with judicial functions wish to impose very severe punishments on wrongdoers, they destroy them with a relatively slow-burning fire; so also, therefore, did the Enemy create unceasing torment for her night and day from her inner organs, by stirring up, so to speak, the fire that was ever smouldering.

107

And while nobly submitting to this affliction, Syncletica did not fail in resolve. On the contrary, the blessed woman continued her struggle against the Enemy. And, at least, by means of her good teachings she still kept healing those wounded by him. And, actually, she continued drawing away from a blood-thirsty lion, as it were, souls that were not wounded. The wounded, moreover, she continued to heal with the saving remedies of the Lord. But some souls she kept safe without any wounds at all; for, by revealing to them the treacherous snares of the Devil, she rendered them free from sin.

108

And the admirable woman used to say that souls dedicated to God must never be careless. The Enemy lies in wait for these souls especially. Indeed, when they are at peace, he gnashes his teeth, and when he is bested, he is vexed, and, withdrawing a little, he keeps watch. And he trips up a person by the very qualities about which he thinks he has no cause for concern. For just as it is impossible for utterly base people not to have even a spark of good, so the opposite holds true for good people; some portion of those engaged in battle lies in opposing camps. Often, at any rate, a person dwells in the midst of every kind of shame and is involved with every kind of intemperance, but nevertheless is merciful. And often among devoted people chastity, fasting, and vigorous discipline are practised, but they are misers and scandalmongers.

109

It is necessary, therefore, not to be negligent in small matters as if they lacked the power to do harm; for water over time has worn away stone. On the one hand, then, the greatest of goods among humans comes to them through divine grace, but, on the other hand, those matters that seem to be small we have been taught to fend off on our own. And so, a person who has done battle with major temptation through grace, but who has scorned minor temptation, will be greatly harmed. For, like a true father, our Lord stretches out his hand when he children are just attempting to walk; and, while rescuing us from any one of the major dangers, he allows us to react on our own to minor ones, showing us by means of these feet of ours, so to speak,[112] that our will is free. For how could the person who is easily overcome in small temptations be on guard in larger ones?

110

Again, on seeing Syncletica gaining strength against him, the Hater of Good was angered. On seeing his own tyranny being destroyed, he devised[113] another kind of evil: he afflicted her organs of speech to cut off her spoken word, thinking in this way to make the women gathered around her go hungry for her inspired words. But even if he had stripped their hearing of her helpful words, in the longer run benefit was conferred, for as the women contemplated[114] her sufferings with their own eyes, they were strengthened in their will; the wounds in her body healed their afflicted souls. It was possible to see the vigilance and healing of those who watched the blessed woman's nobility of soul and patience in suffering.

111

The Enemy, therefore, made the cause of her affliction as follows: after he had inflicted pain in one molar, he caused the gums to become infected immediately. The bone deteriorated; the sore spread through the whole jaw and became the source of infection for the adjacent body parts. Within forty days the bone decayed, and after a period of two months a hole appeared.[115] All the areas round about, then, were blackened, and the bone, its substance perished, was destroyed little by little. Putrefaction and a very foul-smelling stench overpowered her body throughout so that those women who tended her suffered more than she did. They used to withdraw for quite long periods of time, unable to endure the inhuman stench. But when need called, they came near, burning a lot of incense, and again they retired because of the inhuman stench. But the blessed woman saw the Enemy clearly and did not allow any human help at all to be brought to her, demonstrating by this means also her personal courage.[116] Her companions urged her to anoint the offensive places with unguents for the sake of their own weakness. She was not persuaded, however, for she believed that she was diminished in the glorious combat by the help of external agents. And, indeed, her companions did summon a doctor so that, if at all possible, he might in person persuade her to accept treatment. But she, on the contrary, did not permit it, saying: "Why are you holding me back from this noble contest? Why do you search out the visible aspects, sisters,[117] while ignoring the hidden? Why do you fuss about the situation at hand while not looking at the one who is creating it?" And in answer to her the doctor who was there said:[118] "We are not offering medication in the expectation of any healing or relief, but so that we may bury according to custom flesh that is already dead and decayed, lest those present be infected at the same time. For what people offer to the dead, this we also are now doing. I have mixed myrrh and myrtle wine with aloes and am now applying it." She accepted his counsel and tolerated the treatment, more in pity for her companions than anything else, for the indescribable stench was ameliorated by this measure.

112

Who did not shudder at the sight of such an affliction? Who was not helped at the sight of the endurance of the blessed woman? and at the perception of the Enemy's downfall in her? He located the infection in the place from which the saving and ever-so-sweet spring of her discourse gushed forth, and the excessiveness of his cruelty dissipated every comfort. Like a bloodthirsty beast he frightened off all the dedication of her companions in order to tear apart his fallen prey; and yet, in his search for a meal, he became food himself He was caught, as if by a hook, by the weakness of her body; for, on seeing a woman, he was contemptuous, for he failed to recognise her manly will.[119] He perceived that her limbs were diseased; in fact, he was blind, unable to discern her immensely strong mentality. Well, then, for three months she continued to struggle even in this contest. Her body, however, was supported over all by divine power, for what contributed to her body's endurance was diminishing. Malnutrition, then, became a factor; for how could she partake of food when so great an infection and stench held sway? And sleep had also abandoned her, driven away by her sufferings.

113

When her goal of victory and the crown were at hand, she experienced visions: the watchful hovering of angels, the encouragement of holy maidens for her passage, the radiance of ineffable light, and a paradisal realm. And after the vision of these wonders, as if coming to herself, she bade the women present to bear up bravely, and not to be discouraged in the present circumstances. And she said to them: "In three days I shall be separated from my body." And not only this did she reveal, but also the hour of her departure from this world. And when the time had been completed, the blessed Syncletica went off to the Lord, having received from him the kingdom of heaven as a praise for her struggles and praise of our Lord Jesus Christ with the Father and the Holy Spirit forever and ever. Amen.

Lord, God of Hosts,
through the intercession of the Theotokos,
worthy of all praise, my firm hope,
and of the Fathers whose lives I have collected
with enthusiasm and effort,
deem me, a sinner,
worthy to find grace in your sight
according to the judgements which you know.

At this point the words issuing from the Saint Syncletica through the blessed Arsenius of Pegades have been fully recorded exactly according to their proper sequence.

SAINTE SINCLETIQUE

REFERENCES & ABBREVIATIONS
✳

DICTIONARIES

LSJ   H.G. Liddell and R. Scott, *A Greek-English Lexicon*, ed. H. Stuart Jones and R. McKenzie. 9th ed. (Oxford: Clarendon Press, 1940).

Lampe   G.H.W. Lampe, *A Patristic Greek Lexicon* (Oxford: Clarendon Press, 1961).

BAGD   W. Bauer, W. Arndt, F.W. Gingrich, and F.W. Danker, *Greek-English Lexicon of the New Testament and Other Early Christian Literature*. 2nd ed. (Chicago: University of Chicago Press, 1979).

Sophocles   E.A. Sophocles, *Greek Lexicon of the Roman and Byzantine Periods* (Cambridge MA: Harvard University Press; London: Oxford University Press, 1914).

BIBLES

[GREEK]

LXX   *Septuagint*, ed. Alfred Rahlf. 8th ed. (Stuttgart: Württembergische Bibelanstalt, 1935).

NT   *The Greek New Testament*, ed. K. Aland, et al. 3rd ed. (New York: United Bible Societies, 1975).

[LATIN]

Vg   *Biblia Sacra iuxta vulgatam versionem*, ed. Robertus Weber (Stuttgart: Württembergische Bibelanstalt, 1975).

[ENGLISH]

NRSV   *Holy Bible: The New Revised Standard Version* (Nashville: Holman Bible Publishers, 1989).

TEXTS

Migne   J.-P. Migne, *Patrologia Graeca* 28, cols 1488–1557

Alpha. Syn.   *Apophthegmata Patrum*

              1–18: Migne, *Patrologia Graeca* 65, cols. 421–428

              19–27: J.C. Guy, *Recherches sur la tradition grecque des "Apophthegmata Patrum"*, Subsidia hagiographica 36 (Brussels: Société des Bollandistes, 1962), pp. 34–35.

Paul Ev.   Paul Evergetinos, *Collection (Συναγωγή): Collection of the Divinely-Inspired Words and Teachings of the God-bearing and Holy Fathers, Collected From Every Spiritual Writing*, ed. and trans. into modern Greek by Viktor Matthaios (Athens, 1966).

TRANSLATIONS

Migne Latin   The Latin translation accompanying the Greek text in Migne (as above)

Bernard   *Vie de Sainte Synclétique*, trans. Sister Odile Benedicte Bernard, Spiritualité Orientale 9 (Abbaye Notre-Dame de Bellefontaine, 1972).

Castelli   "Pseudo-Athanasius: The Life and Activity of the Holy and Blessed Teacher Syncletica," introd. and trans. Elizabeth A. Castelli in *Ascetic Behaviour in Greco-Roman Antiquity: A Sourcebook*, ed. Vincent L. Wimbush (Minneapolis: Fortress Press, 1990) 265–311.

Paul Ev.   See above under Texts; a translation into modern Greek
            by Viktor Matthaios

Ward   *The Sayings of the Desert Fathers: The Alphabetical Collec-
            tion,* trans. Benedicta Ward. Rev. ed. (Kalamazoo: Cister-
            cian Publications, 1984). s. v. "Syncletica," 230–235.

OTHER ANCIENT SOURCES

Athanasius   Athanasius, *The Life of Antony and the Letter to Mar-
             cellinus,* trans. and introd. Robert C. Gregg (New York:
             Paulist Press, 1980).

Evagrius   Evagrius Ponticus, *The Praktikos and Chapters on Prayer,*
             introd. and trans. John Eudes Bamberger (Kalamazoo:
             Cistercian Publications, 1981).
             Jeremy Driscoll, *The 'Ad Monachos' of Evagrius Ponticus:
             Its Structure and a Select Commentary* Studia Anselmiana
             104 (Rome: Pontificio Ateneo S. Anselmo, 1991).

Gregory   Gregory of Nyssa, *The Life of Saint Macrina,* introd. and
             trans. Kevin Corrigan, Peregrina Translations series
             (Toronto: Peregrina Publishing Co., 1987).

Methodius   Methodius of Olympus, *The Symposium: A Treatise on
             Chastity,* introd. and trans. Herbert Musurillo. Ancient
             Christian Writers 27 (Westminster MD: Newman Press,
             1958).

EVAGRIVS sacri diuina oracula verbi 19 Vnde suis sanctæ præcepta salubria vitæ,
Doctus, et æternæ dogmata legis, erat. Inuicta aduersus dæmonis arma, dabat.

NOTES

✳

1. πολιτεία· ρεγιμεν, i.e., her ascetic way of life. The second καί is either unnecessary or misplaced. The work on Syncletica is not intended to be only a βίος or *vita*; it is intended to be also a description of her πολιτεία. On the meaning and use of πολιτεία, see Tim Vivian's introduction to *Paphnutius, Histories of the Monks of Upper Egypt & The Life of Onnophrius* (Kalamazoo: Cistercian Publications, 1993) 17. In her introduction (265), Castelli states: "Despite its promising title, this fifth-century *vita* (Life) . . . is not primarily a biography. . . ." The title does not, in fact, promise that the work is "primarily" a biography.

2. On the name Syncletica: see Tim Vivian, "Syncletica of Palestine: a Sixth-Century Female Anchorite" *Vox Benedictina* 10: 1 (1993) 27, n. 18. See below, Ch. 4, where she is said to be "named for the heavenly assembly. Yizhar Hirschfeld, *The Judaean Desert Monasteries in the Byzantine Period* (New Haven: Yale University Press, 1992) 247 calls Syncletica of Palestine "the Senator's daughter" as if Syncletica were a title rather than a name. Despite its allegorical connotations, the name, attested as it is in several places, seems genuine.

3. In the first part of Ch. 1, the tenses in Greek are past from the point of view of the writer as he began his work. Cf. epistolary imperfect; see Smyth, *Greek Grammar*, #1942; on ἔδει specifically, the first word in this text, Smyth, #1905, states it may routinely refer to the present.

4. εἶεν one of the few optatives in this work; its use here signals an "unreal" condition, although in general the author's handling of moods and tenses in conditionals is loose.

5. τοῖς πράγμασι=πρακτική, as used by Evagrius. See Guillaumont's introduction to *Praktikos*, 38–63.

6. ἀζήμιον: something on which there is nothing owing.

7. That is to say, as he writes, he preserves for himself the knowledge of Syncletica's life that will help in his own salvation.

8. "charity"=ἀγάπη.

9. ἀσκέω.

10. Another example of Thecla's importance in the ascetic tradition of women; see Castelli, 268ff., n. 12.

11. A term used elsewhere for Paul; see Lampe, s.v. νυμφαγωγός.

12. Both Castelli and Bernard understand this passage differently. παρά plus the accusative can, to be sure, mean "contrary to" as they take it, but it can also mean "according to," as I take it. With this meaning, the passage says simply that sometimes she was forced to eat at the regular times when most people have their meals.

13. In Greek the tense of the main verbs in these last two sentences is present.

14. There is a word play in Greek on κόσμος and κόσμησις.

15. i.e., "simple" or "stripped" of superfluous concerns.

16. The tenses in the Greek are aorist.

17. ἕως τινός = *aliquamdiu* (see Sophocles, s.v. ἕως).

18. Literally "binding together all her joinings" or her "fastenings."

19. cf. Heb 6: 19 where hope, not faith, is the anchor.

20. ἀκτημοσύνη = voluntary poverty, but see below, n. 36.

21. The text has 3 sg. pres. indic. and so could mean "[Scripture] says." The Migne Latin translation takes the 3 sg. as referring to Syncletica, but this does not make sense. I follow Castelli in assuming a textual error for the 3 pl.; Bernard also attributes the quotation to the women.

22. cf. *Alpha. Syn.* 23. For a translation of these excerpts from Syncletica, see Ward. Recent source books on women in religion also include these excerpts but they use Ward's translation; e.g., *Maenads, Martyrs, Matrons, Monastics: A Sourcebook on Women 's Religions in the Greco-Roman World*, ed. Ross S. Kraemer. (Philadelphia: Fortress Press,

1988) 118–22; *Silent Voices, Sacred Lives: Women's Readings for the Liturgical Year*, ed. Barbara Bowe. et al. (New York: Paulist Press, 1992) 97–103.

23. Feminine.

24. i.e., "live chastely in marriage;" the thought demands this interpretation as the Migne Latin translation, Castelli, and Bernard agree.

25. i.e., "chastely in marriage", as above, n. 24.

26. cf. *Alpha Syn.* 2, from the beginning of the chapter.

27. cf. *Alpha. Syn.* from "through our senses". This passage has been inadvertently omitted in Ward, where it should appear between #23 and #24. In Guy's additions it appears as S6, p. 35.

28. cf *Alpha. Syn.* 14.

29. aorist subjunctive, but used with οὐκ – probably an itacism for the future.

30. sexual impurity = πορνεία. This word is frequently translated as "fornication." It often does mean exactly that, but its range of meaning is much wider and so I have decided to use the somewhat awkward expression "sexual impurity" to translate it. See Aline Rousselle, *Porneia: On Desire and the Body in Antiquity*, trans. Felicia Pheasant from the 1983 French original: (Oxford: Basil Blackwell, 1988) 4.

31. See also Athanasius 5 where the expression in the navel of his belly is used in a similar context.

32. cf. *Alpha. Syn.* 18, from "Let us become."

33. That is, by setting a mental apparition against a mental apparition. The comparison with the use of a nail to drive out another nail appears also in Evagrius, *Praktikos* 58.

34. In the literal sense of "drinking party."

35. Water to cut the wine, as was customary in the ancient world.

36. ἀκτημοσύνη, the usual word for the monastic virtue, whereas further down, ἑκουσία πενία is used as a synonym. The distinction between the terms is not as absolute as Castelli indicates (274, n. 46).

37. cf. *Alpha. Syn.* 5, from "Is voluntary poverty."

38. For a similar comparison with cleaning clothes, see Evagrius, *On Prayer* 140.

39. τῷ ἀνδρείῳ φρονήματι: "virile" or "manly" mind, i.e., courageous. Courage was considered a manly virtue, not to be expected of a woman. See below, n. 251.

40. For this common misconception from the Physiologus tradition, see, for example, Pliny, *N.H.* 10: 82.

41. The pronoun is feminine.

42. cf. *Alpha. Syn.* 10, from "and those people too."

43. cf. *Alpha. Syn.* 21 (from "As a treasure"). The Migne text has τόνον which Castelli and I follow; Guy's text (S3, p. 35) has πόνον; hence Ward's translation of 21: "loses all results of its labour" (234).

44. ἀκηδία: "listlessness," "depression," "despondency" are some of modern attempts to translate this term. Here it is a sub-category of γύπη. Evagrius treats them as two distinct vices, whereas in this work λύπη is a general term and ἀκηδία is the specific vice.

45. cf. *Alpha. Syn.* 27, the whole chapter.

46. i.e., "austerities" in the ascetic context.

47. The participle indicates feminine.

48. This chapter incorporates a rhetorical topos. Castelli's n. 101 (p. 284) limits it to "literature concerning female ascetic behaviour," but surely it is used more widely both in pagan and Christian literature. See Averil Cameron, *Christianity and the Rhetoric of Empire*, Ch. 5: "The Rhetoric of Paradox"(Berkeley: University of California Press, 1991), especially 171ff. See also Peter Brown, *The Body and Society: Men, Women, and Sexual Renunciation in Early Christianity* (New York: Columbia University Press, 1988) 327.

49. For the meaning and use of these terms (γνῶσις and πρακτική) in the ascetic context, see A. Guillaumont's introduction to *Evagre le Pontique, Traité pratique ou Le moine*, vol. 1 (Paris: Cerf, 1971) 38–63, and especially 48ff. See also Bamberger: Evagrius Ponticus, *The Praktikos; Chapters on Prayer* and Jeremy Driscoll *The 'Ad Monachos' of Evagrius*

Ponticus: Its Structure and a Select Commentary, II ff.

50. The participle indicates feminine.

51. Castelli (n. 105) compares Evagrius, *Chapters on Prayer* 82. The thought may be comparable, but there is no verbal similarity aside from eagles.

52. The participle indicates feminine.

53. The Migne text has ἔξωθεν here, but the text can be corrected from *Alpha. Syn.* 24.

54. cf. *Alpha. Syn.* 24, from "We must arm ourselves."

55. cf. *Alpha. Syn.* 25, from this sentence through the whole of Ch.

56. The participle indicates feminine.

57. παῖδες ἰατρῶν: "doctors"; see LSJ, s.v. παῖς 3.

58. The text seems to have a problem here. I have read πάντα for πάντας.

59. A line is out of order in the Migne text. Lines 3, 4 and 5 should be in the order 4, 5 and 3.

60. The tenses of the Greek verbs for "tolerate" and "spew" are aorist.

61. cf. *Alpha. Syn.* 1, from "For those who are making."

62. "anger" here translates θυμός. Driscoll consistently translates θυμός as "irascibility" (Evagrius, *Ad Mon.* 30, 35, 36, 98, 100) and, on occasion, Bamberger also translates it in this way, although he more frequently uses "anger." Syncletica seems to use qumoiv and ojrghv as virtual synonyms, as can be seen in the following section. In Ch. 63 τὸ ὀργίζεσθαι appears as an alternative expression.

63. "self-control" translates σωφροσύνη. This term often has the narrower meaning of "chastity," as Castelli renders it here; I think the sense is better served in this passage by the more general meaning.

64. "anger" translates θυμός; "wrath" translates ὀργή.

65. cf. *Alpha. Syn.* 13, from the beginning of the chapter.

66. The participle is feminine.

67. This is an exact quotation of the LXX text.

68. This is also an exact quotation of the LXX text.

69.   Migne (col. 1527, n. 90) reports Cotelier's reading of ὕπνῳ for δείπνῳ, i.e., "sleep" for "banquet."

70.   The participle is feminine.

71.   Note that "you will bend" is future active in Greek and therefore transitive; it does not mean "you will bend yourself."

72.   Bernard has an additional sentence at this point that is not in the Migne text: "Ils en reçoivent des coups, car les démons, se voyant privés de leur propres intruments [sic], les malmènent encore plus" (62).

73.   The Migne text reads "third," but the sense requires "first," as Bernard also concludes.

74.   "On one person, but on all": instead of the dative commonly found after ἐντέλλομαι, the Migne text has πρός and the accusative. I have translated this prepositional phrase as equivalent to the dative, but perhaps it indicates a different meaning: "The Lord did not command love towards one person but towards all." Bernard understands this latter meaning.

75.   μελέτη θανάτου: "a rehearsal of death." Castelli (296, n. 162) points out Plato's use of this expression in Phd. 81a in connection with philosophy. Within the ascetic tradition: Evagrius, *Praktikos* 52 uses this phrase to describe ἀναχώρησις; Methodius also uses this expression in comparing falling asleep from a wakeful state and rising up from a sleeping condition to "a rehearsal of death and resurrection." See Lampe, μελέτη 3.

76.   cf. *Alpha. Syn.* 22, from "Just as it is not possible."

77.   The participles are feminine.

78.   cf. *Alpha. Syn.* 12, the whole chapter. There are more than the usual number of textual variations, although none of them affects the meaning significantly.

79.   Bernard lists four vices here: "les mauvaises pensées, la médisance, le parjure, l'avarice."

80.   In this passage, the metaphorical language is no less "dense"

than a "forest"! The frequent enclosures with quotation marks indicate my attempt to convey the situation where the author seems to be wavering between the image of insects infesting a place and that of wild beasts lurking in forests.

81.   For a lengthy treatment of the term genesis meaning "destiny-at-birth" or "determinism" in the ascetic tradition, see Methodius, 125ff. See also 230, n. 82 where genesis in this context is defined as "the individual destiny as determined by the horoscope cast at one's birth."

82.   *genesis*: in this context is translated by "destiny-at-birth."

83.   The discussion here hinges on two of the meanings of γένεσις: 1. origin, source, beginning, birth, and 2. destiny-at-birth. It also exploits the similarity in Greek of γένεσις and γέννησις (engendering; birth).

84.   See Mt 2: 2.

85.   ὥστε + the infinitive customarily indicates result, but I follow Castelli and Bernard in resorting to a translation that makes purpose the main idea.

86.   The liver as the seat of emotions.

87.   That is, their reason.

88.   ἐγγαστρίμυθος: Castelli and Bernard translate this word as "ventriloquist," but see Lampe, s. v. ἐ. "frequently of women believed to prophesy in this manner;" i.e., women who mouth the words of the demon or divinity possessing them. LSJ also relates this word to women who prophesy. Cf. Acts 16: 16ff.

89.   αὐτοματισμόν: Castelli translates this as "chance;" similarly Bernard uses "hasard," and the Migne Latin "fortuitum rerum eventum." That sense, however, does not seem to suit the context. Lampe (s.v. αὐτοματισμός) gives the meaning of "the automatic working of natural forces." This concept fits more appropriately within a context of predestination.

90.   The participle is feminine.

91.   "to tend," literally "to irrigate."

92.   cf. *Alpha. Syn.* 6, the whole chapter.

93.   cf. *Alpha. Syn.* 4, the whole chapter.

94.   Not in Migne's text, but essential to the meaning.

95.   This expression is the one used by Bernard.

96.   cf. *Alpha. Syn.* 19, from "And many, though on a mountain."

97.   ἐξ αἰτήσεως: the meaning is not clear to me. Castelli has "by means of neglect" (305); Ward has omitted it (232); Bernard has "par permission divine" (88).

98.   The Migne text is faulty at this point and has been supplemented from *Alpha. Syn.* 7.

99.   The text of LXX 68: 30 refers to beggar and in pain, and is quoted accurately in *Alpha. Syn.* 7. In the following sentence, the two states are referred to as a pair (δυάδος). The text we have in Migne has added a third item (*pauper*) and made the next sentence consistent by referring to a triad (τριάδος).

100.   Ward (232) translates Ps 4: 3 ("The Lord hears when I call him"), although *Alpha. Syn.* 7 (Migne 65, col. 424) has the same verse we find here.

101.   cf. *Alpha. Syn.* 7, the whole chapter.

102.   cf. *Alpha. Syn.* 8, from the beginning of the chapter.

103.   The participle is feminine.

104.   cf. *Alpha. Syn.* 16.

105.   cf. *Alpha. Syn.* 15, from "There is also a discipline."

106.   Castelli identifies this vaguely as a "saying from oral tradition" (306, n. 201) and refers to John Cassian *Conference* 1: 20. The introduction to Bernard (XIII) also refers to John Cassian, and notes that this saying is often cited in the Fathers.

107.   χάραγμα: refers to the mark made by the stamp, not to the "die" (χαρακτήρ).

108.   The participle is feminine and the language throughout this chapter is feminine.

109. cf. *Alpha. Syn.* 17; where the language is masculine in this excerpt; e.g., πατρί appears for ματρί.

110. cf. *Alpha. Syn.* 9, the whole chapter.

111. This is present tense in Greek. Two other present tenses appear in the first half of the chapter, which I have also translated as past tenses for consistency.

112. That is, by allowing us to stand on our own two feet.

113. The tense of this verb and of the following "afflicted" is present in Greek.

114. ἐνακενίζουσαι: misprint for ἐνατενίζουσαι.

115. Up to this point in the chapter the tenses of the verbs are present.

116. ἀνδρεία: the usual word for "courage." Castelli translates it as "virility" and Bernard as "virilité". It is true that "courage" is literally a "manly" virtue, but here that connotation is not necessarily at issue. See Ch. 112 below where, in contrast, the distinction between masculine and feminine virtue is clearly referred to. See also above, n. 78.

117. The participles are feminine.

118. The tense in Greek is present.

119. Note the male / female values here clearly denoted in contrast to the previous chapter: ἀνδρεῖος: manly.

Progenie clarus, virtute ANTONIVS ardens,   2   Casta pijs metuet precibus ieiunia, ce iæt
Pauperibus largus, sobrietate amans,   Dæmonis insultus reprimit atq̃, dolos.

SELECT BIBLIOGRAPHY

Acts of Paul and Thecla. In *Fathers of the Third and Fourth Centuries: Apocrypha.* Ed. A. Cleveland Coxe, 487–491. Ante-Nicene Fathers. Vol. 8. New York: Scribner's, 1925.

Alexandre, Monique. *Les nouveaux martyrs.* In *The Biographical Works of Gregory of Nyssa.* Ed. Andreas Spira, 33–70. Patristic Monograph Ser. 12. Cambridge, MA: Philadelphia Patristic Foundation, 1984.

Ancrene Riwle. Trans. M. B. Salu. Intro. Gerard Sitwell. London: Burns and Oates, 1955.

Athanasius. *First Letter to Virgins,* Trans. David Brakke. In David Brakke. *Athanasius and the Politics of Asceticism,* Appendix A, 274–291. Oxford: Clarendon, 1995.

———. *The Life of Antony and The Letter to Marcellinus.* Trans. and intro. Robert C. Gregg. New York: Paulist, 1980.

———. *On Virginity. Athanasius and the Politics of Asceticism.* Trans. David Brakke. In David Brakke. *Athanasius and the Politics of Asceticism,* Appendix C, 303–309. Oxford: Clarendon, 1995.

Baronius, Caesar. *Martyrologium Romanum.* Antwerp: Plantin, 1589.

Bible. *The New Oxford Annotated Bible.* Ed. Bruce Metzger and Roland E. Murphy. 1991; rpt. New York: Oxford University Press, 1994.

Brakke, David. "The Authenticity of the Ascetic Athanasiana." *Orientalia* 63 (1994) 17–56.

Brock, Sebastian. *The Luminous Eye.* Kalamazoo: Cistercian Publications, 1992.

Brown, Peter. *The Body and Society.* New York: Columbia University Press, 1988.

Bulteau, Dom. *Essai de l'histoire monastique d'Orient,* 168–171. Paris: Louis Billaine, 1680.

Butler, Alban. *Lives of the Saints.* Vol. 1. London, 1756. Published anonymously.

Canons from the Council of Gangra. Intro. and trans. O. Larry Yarborough. In *Ascetic Behaviour in Late Antiquity,* ed. Vincent L. Wimbush, 448–455. Minneapolis: Fortress, 1990.

Cassian, John. *John Cassian: The Conferences.* Trans. and annotated Boniface Ramsey. Ancient Christian Writers 57. New York and Mahwah, NJ: Paulist, 1997.

Castelli, Elizabeth A. "Mortifying the Body, Curing the Soul: Beyond Ascetic Dualism in The Life of Saint Syncletica." *Differences* 4:2 (1992) 134–153.

——. "Virginity and Its Meaning for Women's Sexuality in Early Christianity." *Journal of Feminist Studies in Religion* 2:1 (1986) 61–88.

Chadwick, Owen. *Western Asceticism.* Library of Christian Classics. Vol. 12. Philadelphia: Westminster, 1958.

Challoner, Richard. *Wonders of God in the Wilderness.* London: n.p., 1755.

Clark, Elizabeth A. "Ascetic Renunciation and Feminine Advancement: A Paradox of Late Ancient Christianity." *Anglican Theological Review* 63 (1981) 240–257. Rpt. in *Ascetic Piety and Women's Faith: Essays on Late Ancient Christianity,* 175–208. Lewiston, NY: Mellen, 1986.

——. "Authority and Humility: A Conflict of Values in Fourth-Century Female Monasticism." *Byzantinishe Forschungen* 9 (1985) 17–33. Rpt. in *Ascetic Piety and Women's Faith: Essays on Late Ancient Christianity,* 209–228. Lewiston, NY: Mellen, 1986.

——. "Devil's Gateway and Bride of Christ: Women in the Early Christian World." In *Ascetic Piety and Women's Faith: Essays on Late Ancient Christianity,* 23–60. Lewiston, NY: Mellen , 1986.

——. "Introduction." In *The Life of Melania, the Younger by Gerontius.* Trans. and commentary by Elizabeth A. Clark, 1–24. New York and Toronto: Mellen, 1984.

Gillian Clark, *Women in Late Antiquity: Pagan and Christian Life-Style* Oxford: Clarendon Press, 1993.

Clement of Alexandria. *The Instructor*. In *The Writings of Clement of Alexandria*. Trans. William Wilson. Vol. 1, 113–346. Ante-Nicene Christian Library. Ed. Alexander Roberts and James Donaldson. Vol. 4. Edinburgh: T. and T. Clark, 1880.

Corrigan, Kevin. "Syncletica and Macrina: Two Early Lives of Women Saints." *Vox Benedictina* 6:03 (1989) 241–256.

D'Andilly, Robert Arnauld. *Vies des saints pères*. Vol. 3, 91–156. Paris: n.p., 1676.

Deferrari, Roy J. Deferrari. "Introduction." In *Early Christian Biographies*. Ed. Roy J. Deferrari. The Fathers of the Church. Vol. 15. Washington, DC: Fathers of the Church, 1952.

Driscoll, Jeremy. *The Ad Monachos of Evagrius Ponticus: Its Structure and a Select Commentary*. Rome: Studia Anselmiana, 1991.

——. "Spiritual Progress in the Works of Evagrius Ponticus." In *Spiritual Progress: Studies in the Spirituality of Late Antiquity and Early Monasticism*. Ed. Jeremy Driscoll and Mark Sheridan, 47–84. Rome: Studia Anselmiana, 1994.

Elliott, Alison Goddard. *Roads to Paradise: Reading the Lives of the Early Saints*. Hanover: University Press of New England, 1987.

Elm, Susanna. "Evagrius Ponticus' *Sententiae ad Virginem*." *Dumbarton Oaks Papers* 45 (1991) 97–120.

——. "The *Sententiae ad Virginem* by Evagrius Ponticus and the Problem of Early Monastic Rules." *Augustinianum* 30 (1990) 393–404.

Eusebius. *The History of the Church*. Trans. G. A. Williamson. Rev., ed. and intro. Andrew Louth. 1965; rpt. London: Penguin, 1989.

Evagrius Ponticus. *The Mind's Long Journey to the Holy Trinity: The Ad Monachos of Evagrius Ponticus*. Trans. and notes Jeremy Driscoll. Collegeville, MN: Liturgical Press, 1993.

—. *The Praktikos and Chapters on Prayer*. Trans. and intro. John Eudes Bamberger. Kalamazoo: Cistercian Publications, 1981.

—. *Sententiae ad Virginem*. Trans. Scott Richardson. Saint Johnís University, Collegeville, MN. June 30, 1996. Unpublished.

Fernandez, Domiciano. "La spiritualité mariale chez les pères de l'Èglise. (Vierge)." *Dictionnaire de spiritualité* 10, cols. 423–440. Paris: Beauchesne, 1980.

Forman, Mary, "Amma Syncletica: A Spirituality of Experience." *Vox Benedictina* 10: 2 (Winter 1993) 199–237. This article appears also in an abridged form in *On Pilgrimage: the Best of Ten Years of Vox Benedictina*, ed. Margot King (Toronto: Peregrina, 1994) 259–282.

Grabar, André. *Christian Iconography*. A. W. Mellon Lectures in the Fine Arts, 1961. Bollingen Ser. 35. 1968; rpt. Princeton: Princeton University Press, 1980.

Graef, Hilda. *Mary: A History of Doctrine and Devotion*. 1963; rpt. Westminster MD: Christian Classics, 1985.

Gregory of Nyssa. *The Life of Macrina*. Trans. and intro. Kevin Corrigan. Toronto: Peregrina Publishing Co., 1995.

—. *On Virginity*. In *Saint Gregory of Nyssa Ascetical Works*. Trans. Virginia Woods Callahan, 6–75. The Fathers of the Church. 1967; rpt. Washington, DC.: Catholic University of America Press, 1990.

Guerin, Paul. *Les petits Bollandistes: vies des saints*. 7th ed. Vol. 1. Paris: Bloud et Barral, 1880.

Hadot, Pierre. *Philosophy as a Way of Life: Spiritual Exercises from Socrates to Foucault*. Ed. and intro. Arnold I. Davidson. Trans. Michael Chase. Oxford UK and Cambridge MA: Blackwell, 1995.

Hausherr, Irénée. "L'origine de la théorie orientale des huit pèchés capitaux." *Orientalia Christiana* 30.86 (1933) 164–175.

—. *Spiritual Direction in the Early Christian East*. Trans. Anthony P. Gythiel. Kalamazoo: Cistercian Publications, 1990.

Hélyot, Pierre Hippolyte. *Histoire des ordres monastiques religieux et militaires et des congregations seculières.* Vol. 1. Paris: Nicola Gosselin, 1714.

Hippolytus. *Hippolytus: A Text for Students.* Trans., intro., commentary and notes Geoffrey J. Cuming Bramcote Notts: Grove, 1976.

Hopper, Vincent Foster. *Medieval Number Symbolism: Its Sources, Meaning, and Influence on Thought and Expression.* 1938; rpt. Folcroft, 1975.

Irenaeus of Lyons. *Adversus haereses.* In *The Writings of Irenaeus.* Trans. Alexander Roberts and W. H. Rambout. 2 vol. Edinburgh: T. and T. Clark, 1880.

Jerome. *Letter to Eustochium* (EP. 22). In *St. Jerome: Letters and Select Works.* Trans. W. H. Fremantle. Nicene and Post-Nicene Fathers. 2nd. ser. Vol. 6. Edinburgh: T. and T. Clark; Grand Rapids, MI: Wm. B. Eerdmans, rpt. 1989. 22–41.

John Climacus. *The Ladder of Divine Ascent.* Trans. Colm Luibheid and Norman Russell. Classics of Western Spirituality. New York: Paulist, 1982.

Krautheimer, Richard. *Early Christian and Byzantine Architecture.* 3rd. rev. ed. Pelican History of Art. New York: Penguin, 1981.

Lampe, G.W.H., ed. *A Patristic Lexicon.* Oxford: Clarendon, 1961.

Liddell, Henry George and Scott, Robert, comp. *Greek-English Lexicon.* Rev. ed. Henry Stuart Jones with Roderick McKenzie. 2 vol. Oxford: Clarendon, 1925.

Lowrie, Walter. *Monuments of the Early Church,* 1901. Rev. ed. rpt. as *Art in the Early Church.* 1947; rpt. New York: Norton, 1969.

Matericon: Compilation of the Spiritual Direction Given by Father Isaiah to the Holy Nun Theodora. English translation by the Sisters of the Orthodox Monastery of the Transfiguration, Ellwood City, PA: n.d. Unpublished.

Methodius of Olympus. *The Symposium: A Treatise on Chastity.* Trans. and notes Herbert Musurillo. Westminster, MD: Newman, 1958.

Miller, Patricia Cox. "The Blazing Body: Ascetic Desire in Jerome's

Letter to Eustochium." *Journal of Early Christian Studies.* 1:1 (1993): 21–45.

—. "Desert Asceticism and The Body from Nowhere." *Journal of Early Christian Studies.* 2:2 (1994): 137–153.

——. "Dreaming the Body: An Aesthetics of Asceticism." In *Asceticism*. Ed. Vincent Wimbush and Richard Valantasis, 281–300. New York: Oxford, 1995.

——. "The Two Gregorys and Ascetic Dreaming." In *Dreams in Late Antiquity: Studies in the Imagination of a Culture*, 232–249. Princeton: Princeton University Press, 1994.

Montfaucon, Bernard de. *Bibliotheca Coisliniana*. Paris: Guerin and Robustel, 1715.

Murray, Robert. *Symbols of Church and Kingdom: A Study in Early Syriac Tradition*. London: Cambridge University Press, 1975.

Natalibus, Petrus de. *Catalogus sanctorum*. Lyons: Jacques Sacon, December 1514.

Nicephorus Callixtus. *Ecclesiasticae historiae*. Patrologia Graeca 146. Paris: J.-P. Migne, 1865.

Nugent, M. Rosamond. *Portrait of the Consecrated Woman in Greek Christian Literature of the First Four Centuries*. Catholic University of America Patristic Studies Vol. 69. Washington, DC.: Catholic University of America Press, 1941.

Origen. *Commentaire sur l'evangile selon Matthieu*. Intro., trans. and notes Robert Girod. Vol. 1. Sources chrétiennes 162. Paris: Cerf, 1970.

—. *On First Principles. Origen: An Exhortation to Martyrdom, Prayer, First Principles: Book IV, Prologue to the Commentary on the Song of Songs, Homily XXVII on Numbers*. Trans. and intro. Rowan A. Greer. New York: Paulist, 1979.

Pachomian Koinonia. Trans. with intro. Armand Veilleux. 3 vol. Kalamazoo: Cistercian Publications, 1980.

"Pelagia." *Holy Women of the Syrian Orient*. Trans. Sebastian P. Brock and Susan Ashbrook Harvey, 40–62. Berkeley: University of California Press, 1987.

Piolin, Paul. *Supplément aux vies des saints et spécialement au Petits Bollandistes*. Vol. 1. Paris: Bloud et Barral, 1885.

Pseudo-Athanasius. *The Life and Regimen of the Blessed and Holy Teacher Syncletica*. Trans., intro. and notes Elizabeth Bryson Bongie. Toronto: Peregrina Publishing Co., 1995.

———. "Pseudo-Athanasius: The Life and Activity of the Holy and Blessed Teacher Syncletica." Trans. and notes Elizabeth A. Castelli. In *Ascetic Behaviour in Greco-Roman Antiquity: A Sourcebook*. Ed. Vincent L. Wimbush, 265–311. Minneapolis: Fortress, 1990.

———. *Vita et gesta sanctae beataeque magistrae Syncleticae*/ Βιος και Πολιτεια της αγιας και μακαριας Διδασκαλου Συγκλητινς. *Patrologia Graeca* 28, cols. 1485–1558. Paris: J.-P. Migne, 1887.

Rassart-Debergh, Maguerite. "L'Art des fils des Pharaons." In *Déserts chrétiens d'Egypte*. Pierre Miquel, Antoine Guillaumont, Maguerite Rassart-Debergh, Philippe Bridel and Adalbert de Vogüé, 67–193. Nice: Myriam Orban, 1993.

———. *La vie quotidienne des pères du désert en Egypte au IVe siècle* (Paris, 1990).

Regnault, Lucien. "Introduction." In *Vie de Sainte Synclétique et Discours de salut d'une vierge*. Trans. Odile Bénédicte Bernard and J. Bouvet, 7–19. Spiritualité Orientale 9. Abbaye Notre-Dame de Bellefontaine, 1972.

Rosweyde, Heribert. *De vita et verbis seniorum. (Vitae Patrum)*. Antwerp: Officina Plantin, 1615.

The Sayings of the Desert Fathers. 1975. Rpt. as *The Desert Christian: Sayings of the Desert Fathers, the Alphabetical Collection*. Trans. and foreword Benedicta Ward. New York: Macmillan, 1980.

Schiller, Gertrud. *Iconography of Christian Art*. Trans. Janet Seligman. Vol. 1. Greenwich, CT: New York Graphic Society, 1971.

Sedulius. *Epistola ad Macedonium. Sedulii opera omnia.* Recensuit et commentario critico instruxit Iohannes Huemer. Vindobonae: C. Geroldi filium bibliopolam Academiae, 1885. 1–13.

Sichem, Christoffel van. *'t schat der Zielen.* Amsterdam: Preter and P[aets], 1648.

Soler, Josep. "Les Mères du désert et la maternité spirituelle." *Collectanea Cisterciensia* 48 (1986) 235–250.

Springer, Carl P.E. *The Gospel As Epic in Late Antiquity: the Paschale Carmen of Sedulius.* Leiden: E. J. Brill, 1988.

Stewart, Columba. *Cassian the Monk.* New York: Oxford University Press, 1998.

Topping, Eva Catafygiotu, *Saints and Sisterhood; the Lives of 48 Holy Women* (Minneapolis: 1990) 95–101.

Vivian, Tim. "Introduction." In *Histories of the Monks of Upper Egypt and the Life of Onnophrius.* Trans. by Tim Vivian, 17–70. Kalamazoo: Cistercian Publications, 1993.

—. "Syncletica of Palestine: A Sixth-Century Female Anchorite." *Vox Benedictina* 10:1 (1993) 9–37.

Weitzmann, Kurt, ed. *Age of Spirituality: Late Antique and Early Christian Art, Third to Seventh Century. Catalogue of the exhibition at The Metropolitan Museum of Art, November 19, 1977–February 12, 1978.* New York: The Metropolitan Museum of Art and Princeton University Press, 1979.

Wisdom of the Desert Fathers: Systematic Sayings from the Anonymous Series of the Apophthegmata Patrum. Trans. and intro. Benedicta Ward. Fairacres, Oxford: SLG, 1975.

ILLUSTRATIONS

Cover image: Saint Felicitas mater, from Mathew Rader, *Bavaria sancta* (1624, 1627). Engravings by Raphael Sadeler I (1560–1632) and II II (saec. XVI). See Holsten, p. 284, items 228–240. Verso in ink: P. Mariett 1670.

p. 4 Sancta Syncletica, from *'tBosch der eremyten ende ermitinnen, van Agypten ende Palestinen,* met figuren van Abraham Blommaert. Met cort verhael van eens yders leven ghetrocken uyt het Vadersboeck. 'tHantvverpen: Hieronymus Verdussen, 1689. By courtesy, Arca artium, St. John's University, Collegeville MN)

p. 70 S. Syncletique, from *Les vies des ss. pères des déserts, et des saint solitaries d'orient et d'occident.* Anvers: Chez Pierre Brunel, 1724

p. 74 Sanctus Evagrius, from *Solitudo, sive vitae patrum eremicolarum Solitvdo, sive vitae patrvm eremicolarum;* per antiquissimu[m] Patrem D. Hieronimu[m] eorundem primarium olim conscripta. Iam vero primum aeneis laminis, idq[ue] Ioannis et Raphael Sadeler, fratru[m] impensis sculpt. & excusa, [s.l. s.n], [159-?]. By courtesy, Arca artium, St. John's University, Collegeville MN.

p. 84 Sanctus Antonius, from *Solitudo, sive vitae patrum eremicolarum Solitvdo, sive vitae patrvm eremicolarum;* per antiquissimu[m] Patrem D. Hieronimu[m] eorundem primarium olim conscripta. Iam vero primum aeneis laminis, idq[ue] Ioannis et Raphael Sadeler, fratru[m] impensis sculpt. & excusa, [s.l. s.n], [159-?]. By courtesy, Arca artium, St. John's University, Collegeville MN.